SOUTH

6/40   IX II   2004 EH TOUR   ✓

N/13^   1562   S/1

PHILIP II

1563
1574

Palace Administrative Center, College,
Seminary, Monastery, Church,
Mausoleum.

The Royal Monastery of San Lorenzo de
El Escorial

José Luis Sancho

The Royal Monastery of San Lorenzo de

El Escorial

R S

REALES SITIOS DE ESPAÑA

© PATRIMONIO NACIONAL, 2002

Text: José Luis Sancho Gaspar

Translation: Philip Knight

Revision: Laura Suffield

Photographs: Patrimonio Nacional / Félix Lorrio

Aldeasa / José Barea

N.I.P.O.: 006-02-008-7

I.S.B.N.: 84-7120-318-9

Depósito Legal: M-25669-2002

Co-ordination and production: ALDEASA

Design and layout: La Mar

Film-maker: Lucam

Printer: Brizzolis

Front cover photograph: José Barea

Royal Library. Main Room or Room of the Printed Books, 1586-1591

Pellegrino Tibaldi: frescoes. Juan de Herrera: design of the bookshelves

Antonio Santucci: armillary sphere, ca. 1582

Printed in Spain

Preface

Patrimonio Nacional is the organisation which administers State property for use by the Crown for representative functions specified by the Constitution and Spanish Law.

These properties are a group of palaces, monasteries and convents of royal foundation. They are of outstanding historical, artistic and cultural importance, but above all of great symbolic value. The Royal Palaces of Madrid, El Pardo, Aranjuez, San Ildefonso and La Almudaina are still used as residences and for the ceremonial reasons for which they were originally built centuries ago. In them, His Majesty the King exercises his solemn functions as Chief of State, particularly in the Madrid Royal Palace, which has the greatest symbolic value as official Royal Residence.

In conjunction with these functions, the buildings and other properties which make up Patrimonio Nacional have a specific cultural role which they fulfil through being open to public, as well as being available for study and research.

Both the buildings and the Royal Spanish Collections (covering 27 different areas, from fans to tools and including silver, paintings, tapestries, furniture, musical instruments, clocks, etc) have characteristics which makes Patrimonio Nacional a unique cultural institution. These include way these works of art and objects were used (given that they still have a symbolic functional significance); their historical importance as objects which were specially commissioned, purchased or given for their location; their uniqueness, in that no replicas or imitations have been made of them; and their extraordinary artistic, historic and symbolic value.

Understanding these features will allow the visitor to appreciate that Patrimonio Nacional is much more than a museum.

The Spanish Royal Palaces are surrounded by green spaces, currently covering around 20,500 hectares. Of these, around 500 are flower and vegetable gardens and 20,000 forest. The forested areas are divided between El Pardo, La Herrería and Riofrío and can in part be visited by the public. Their ecological importance within the Mediterranean forest type (of which they mostly consist) is well known, and should not be overshadowed by the monuments which they surround.

The royal monasteries and convents are still occupied by their founding orders, with the exception of San Lorenzo de El Escorial, which, as a consequence of the 19th-century disentailments, passed from the Hieronymite Order to the Augustinians. These foundations have a particular importance in the history of Spain, as they owe their origins to royal patronage.

In addition to a cultural purpose, these buildings are open to the public with the intention of allowing every Spanish person to appreciate something of their symbolic value, to identify with them and feel himself or herself heir to the vast historic and cultural patrimony constituted by the properties which come under the heading of Patrimonio Nacional.

Created over the centuries by the Crown, their influence on the cultural identity of Spain has been and continues to be a decisive one.

Index

MICHEL-ANGE HOUASSE

View of the Monastery of El Escorial, c.1720.

Patrimonio Nacional. Palace of La Moncloa.

Introduction

Within the context of European architecture, Spain has never perhaps received deserved attention, however, a visit to El Escorial is considered essential, given its unique late-Renaissance combination of Flemish and Italian elements used in the construction of an unusual building typologically: that of the palace-monastery. From the Spanish point of view, the importance of the building itself is combined with its role as a model for a uniquely Spanish form of architectural classicism. This national and classicising aspect accounts for the attempts made from various ideological viewpoints in the 20th century to use the Escorial as the starting point for the creation of a late, historicising mode.

To the architectural interest of the building we should add the importance of its contents, which largely date from its earliest phase. This is the period of the creation of the Library, the first major one of its kind to be sponsored by the Spanish monarchy, while the installation of the most important paintings, which together form a veritable museum, dates from the period of Philip IV. Many of the more important ones were subsequently transferred to the Prado Museum, primarily in 1837 and 1939 as records indicate.

Without diminishing its artistic significance, El Escorial represents an extraordinary historical legacy as the place particularly associated with its founder, Philip II, and as the supreme realization of the ideals of the Catholic Monarchy. It is important to emphasise that El Escorial is not simply a museum or a tourist monument but is rather a living institution which, under the patronage of His Majesty the King and the administration of Patrimonio Nacional, continues to fulfil its statutory functions as a pantheon, a college and a monastery.

History

JUAN PANTOJA DE LA CRUZ
Philip II, c. 1590-98 (detail).
Main Room or Room of the
Printed Books.
Library

ANONYMOUS
Map of Europe (detail).
Coloured engraving, 16th-century.
Galería de Paseo. King's Quarters. King's House.

There were two principal reasons for the creation of El Escorial. The first was a funerary one in that the death of Charles V called for the erection of a tomb worthy of that monarch. After weighing up a number of specific options, Charles V opted in favour of entrusting the matter to his son and successor. The other reason, or rather a pretext or added incentive, was as an act of thanksgiving for the victory of Saint Quentin which had taken place on August 10, 1557, the day of the festival of San Lorenzo (Saint Lawrence). If we bear in mind that the fortunate victor was a Spaniard, the unusual and anecdotal dedication of the monastery acquires other, equally plausible motives viewed from the standpoint of an arch defender of orthodoxy as was Philip II.

Recent precedents pointed to the Royal Chapel at Granada as the ideal burial place for the emperor. There were buried his grandparents Isabel and Ferdinand of the Trastámara dynasty, as well as his father, Philip the Fair, who introduced the Habsburg dynasty to Spain. But in this and other aspects, the court had not only abandoned Granada for Castile, its natural headquarters in the network of kingdoms within the

(Left)
Antechamber of Philip II
from the West Wall.
King's Quarters.
King's House.
(Right)
Funerary urns.
Pantheon of the Kings.

peninsula, but it had also embarked on a political project of inevitably representational consequences; the promotion of the capital city. Guided by the new Renaissance concept of exclusive monarchical territory, the establishment in one place of the previously itinerant court likewise entailed a fixed burial place in terms which went beyond Charles' mandate. Thus, the very nature of the promotion of the capital city involved re-orientating the issue of the imperial tomb towards that of dynastic continuity.

The choice of Madrid as the capital city combined with its role as the perfect setting for the monastery to carry out the wishes of Charles V. At the end of 1561, with the royal administrative machine already located in Madrid, not only was the location of the foundation decided but, in addition, the initial generalised design was quickly adapted to its particular characteristics. In order to fully realise his intentions, Philip II looked back to the old concept of a monastery-palace, but with an increasingly systematic programme which, within the overall context of the monastic image, indicated the construction of a modern State.

Juxtaposed against the Hieronymite monastery, an already traditional type used by the Spanish monarchy, different elements such as the Pantheon, the Royal Residence and Royal Libraries, the School and the Seminary would make up a vast independent whole, unparalleled in architectural planning. Their complexity and grandeur would represent a major qualitative step forward compared with the immediate precedent of Yuste, the modest retreat of the Emperor who died there in 1558 as his son was assessing possible locations for a similar place of retreat of his own.

In more than one sense, Philip II reveals himself through this huge enterprise to be a magnified echo of his father, whose late aspirations he reinterpreted from an identical Counter-Reformist standpoint but on a

Anton van Dashorst Mor, called Antonio Moro

Philip II, c. 1557.

Portrait Room. King's Quarters. King's House.

material level and with a type of unified symbolism which was unknown even in Tridentine Italy.

The major part of construction took place gradually between 1562 and 1595, by which time the sovereign only had three years left to live. This was his final retreat, giving rise to a false or exaggerated image of a 'rey oculto' (hidden king).

The maintenance of the original specifications and, at least with regard to the Habsburgs, the memory of the founder, guaranteed the survival of the monastery as an institution until the sale of church lands by Mendizábal in the 19th century. While Philip III initiated the project of the Monarchs' Pantheon, Philip IV completed it. In addition, he contributed an outstanding selection of pictures which Velázquez was responsible for organising in 1656. Charles II's contribution was particularly important, as he had to repair the substantial damage caused by the devastating fire of 1671, and he enriched the monastery with important examples of late Baroque art such as *La Sagrada Forma* (The Sacred Form) by Claudio Coello (1685-90) or the frescoes by Luca Giordano (1692-94).

Following the change of dynasty, there was a certain move away from the concept of the palace-monastery, which may even have endangered its function as a royal pantheon. However, under Charles III, El Escorial not only acquired the unexpected status of classicising architectural prototype but also from 1767 onwards, with the urbanisation of the town, we see the emergence of a new 'real sitio' (royal residence). In addition to completing the enclosure of the terrace known as La Lonja, the two small palaces called the Casita del Princípe and the Casita del Infante were built. Within the context of this symbolic and functional modernising, it is not surprising that Charles IV undertook the updating of part of the building now known as the Palace of the Bourbons.

The monastery was the scene of the so-called "El Escorial Conspiracy" in which the party supporting Ferdinand hatched complex plots against the favourite Godoy and his august protectors. The onset of the Napoleonic wars signalled the start of the most dramatic period for the monastery. Although the ultimate effects of the conflict on the collections were very serious, they were far short of the widespread impression that the site had been totally ravaged.

View of the north-east of the Monastery and the surrounding land
from Mount Abantos, lit up at night.

(Left)
The King's Room, formerly
the Bedroom of the Infantas'
Quarter.
Palace of the Bourbons.
(Right)
The Passageway between
the Eighth and Ninth
Chambers.
Pantheon of the Infantes,
1862-88.

The three most important pictures to be removed, all painted by Raphael, were returned in better condition. Having been sent to Paris in 1813, they were transferred from panel to canvas. On the orders of Joseph Bonaparte, the Royal Library merged with the Royal Library of Madrid at the new premises of the latter. While it is true that important pieces of goldsmiths' work disappeared at this time, this was not only due to looting by the French but also to the lack of diligence shown by the collection's custodians in failing to emulate other ecclesiastical institutions and adopt appropriate preventative measures.

The restoration of El Escorial as both an institution and a building reflected the restoration of Ferdinand VII as absolute monarch. The 'ancien régime' having been left behind, only one of the functions remained from the system which Philip II had used to structure his foundation – the royal burial place (as well as its role as a royal residence). In 1837, with the monastery closed and the community of monks disbanded, the monastery building reverted to the Crown who made vain attempts to find a lasting solution, ensuring the upkeep of the building but also protecting the use of the pantheon. This now included a second pantheon for the Infantes, constructed at the behest of Isabel II. However, it was not completed until 1888 and during the first Republic, under the presidency of Emilio Castelar, it became the subject of a curious plan to convert it into a National Pantheon, after the Madrid church of San Francisco el Grande had been rejected for this purpose.

Meanwhile, El Escorial had acquired the status of "eighth wonder of the world", as evidenced by visits from so many illustrious travellers. Above all as a result of the railway that linked the town and monastery with the capital from 1861 onwards, it quickly became an essential stop for the ever-growing phenomenon of mass tourism.

The Restoration of Alfonso XII also implied the re-establishment of El Escorial as a monastic foundation through an agreement with the Augustinians in 1885 which paved the way for the gradual recovery of its original statutory aims and spirit.

During the Civil War, the monastic treasures did not suffer any important losses except some isolated cases of precious objects, for example, the Virgin of Saint Pius V.

Under the Franco regime, the building became the object of a third doctrinal restoration with the clearly stated aim of political appropriation through which Madrid became the city of 'Los Escoriales'. Whereas the celebration in 1963 of the fourth centenary of the commencement of the project still showed traces of neo-traditionalist manipulation, the celebration in 1986 of the anniversary of its completion adopted neutral guidelines of simply a historical and artistic nature, the only way of approaching the monument, now no longer vulnerable to ideological interpretations. Both inside and outside Spain, renewed scholarly interest in El Escorial has reached quantitative and qualitative levels which would have been unthinkable only a few decades ago.

The construction process

Model of the structure of the
spire of one of the towers (detail).
Museum of Architecture.

South-east Corner with the
Prior's Tower seen from the
balustrade of the dome of
the Basilica.

An intensive search for the appropriate location took place between 1558 and 1561. Despite the lack of a specifically designated space, this involved the drawing up of initial designs. At the beginning of 1561, these were already being discussed and, at the end of that same year, with the site having been chosen, underwent modification according to key requirements of the project. Thus, a process of trial and error or various approaches, which not only met the requirements of the project but were also in line with the personal tastes of the monarch (an architectural enthusiast), resulted in the emergence of the "universal design" (*traza universal*) by Juan Bautista de Toledo. The architect had worked in Rome in the service of Michelangelo and brought to the Spanish court the new classicising language which culminates here in El Escorial.

In 1562, when Juan Bautista de Toledo made a scale model of what can be termed the final plan, which was already underway, he suffered his first professional setback. As well as opening the floodgates of Italian interference, this took away his leading role in the eyes of his Spanish colleagues. The doubtful Philip II began to re-orientate the project towards a joint scheme. Not content with criticising Toledo's church, Francesco Paciotto made an alternative and very different proposal. A 'Council of Architecture', paradoxically made up of technically unqualified members, tried to incorporate these suggestions into the 'universal design'. Two years later there was a redrafting of proposals which combined Paciotto's plans for the church with those of Gaspar de Vega for the building as a whole. According to Marías y Bustamante, between 1563 and 1567, Juan Bautista de Toledo attempted to incorporate Paciotto's observations in three consecutive projects.

Meanwhile a fundamental change of plan meant that substantial modifications had to be made to Toledo's edifice. In 1564, following a decision to double the number of monks from fifty to a hundred, it was agreed that the capacity of the building should be increased accordingly and the whole building was now given four floors, rather than only in the rear section as previously.

According to Father Sigüenza, it was the constructor, Friar Antonio de Villacastín, rather than Toledo, who was responsible for issuing the order to double the façade without altering the 1562 design. But there is serious doubt regarding the resultant "contest of ideas". Rodríguez Robledo has an unusual viewpoint here: within the historical debate as to whether the master builders were the co-designers of El Escorial, he attributes the order to an exchange of letters between the monk, the monarch and Pedro de Tolosa although the measure was originally inspired by Prior Juan de Huete.

It is known that Rodrigo Gil de Hontañón, exponent of a different kind of Renaissance architecture, provided the solution that was actually accepted and which apparently matched Toledo's sentiments. It is surprising that the acquiescence of the architect to levelling the height of the building did not become evident earlier in the form of a suggestion of his own, either within or outside the context of the contest.

Immediately following the death of Juan Bautista de Toledo in 1567, experts in Italy were directly consulted for the first time regarding the design of the basilica. Another consultation took place four years later. In 1567, a confused void had resulted, leading to the emergence of the Cantabrian Juan de Herrera as the head of construction and of the planned alterations (in spite of a great deal of interference). At that time, he was not an experienced architect.

ICONOGRAPHIA MONASTERII DIVI LAVRENTII A PHILIPO II. HISPANIARVM REGE PROPE ESCVRIALE EXTRVCTI.

In accordance with the order of priorities set out in the foundation statutes and with the actual image of this type of construction, work started on the monastery section of the building. The years 1571, 1572 and 1575 saw the completion of the main part of the monastery and the beginning of work on the Casa del Rey (The King's House) and the Church respectively.

From 1579 onwards, Philip II redirected this huge endeavour towards a greater emphasis on three elements – the Library, the Seminary and the School. The last stone was put in place in 1584, made of gold, according to popular tradition, as there was no granite left. However, work on the church did not finish until two years later. The church was consecrated in 1595. By then, the whole project had been virtually completed although some decorative work continued subsequently including such important elements as the sculptural groups on the royal cenotaphs.

The identity of the architects, the style and the overall symbolism of the monastery has generated much sterile debate, since it is impossible to reduce such a varied architectural achievement to simple terms. Further-

PEDRO DE VILLAFRANCA
Iconographia Monasterii Divi
Laurentii…
Descripción breve del
Monasterio de S. Lorenzo
El Real de El Escorial.
Madrid, 1657.

more, the compositional complexity has been accentuated by a succession of complex modifications. In addition, the King's taste (very much influenced by his "very happy trip" through Italy, the Empire and the Low Countries when he was still prince in the company of Juan de Herrera and his retinue) was a determining factor in the inclusion of Flemish elements such as the tall spires and the high slate roofs. Although the 1562 design was maintained, albeit with serious shortcomings, the changes of plan and of architect characterized a flexible project in which identifying the exponents is a very risky task. Toledo's prestige arose mainly from his role as assistant to Michelangelo in the Vatican, a phase that has not yet been fully researched. After Toledo's death, his artistic merit was generally understated to the convenient and automatic benefit of those who continued his work, although their output cannot be remotely compared with that of Toledo.

South-east corner: spire of the lantern and roofs of the four smaller cloisters of the Monastery, seen from the dome of the Basilica.

As Javier Ribera pointed out, the greatest injustice done to Toledo was the systematic way in which it was considered that all his work was rejected following his death without allowing for his ideas to persist. This appears absurd in the light of architectural practice from any age, including the current one. Toledo was not solely responsible for the general layout: while he drew up the main part of the design, Herrera seems to have been in charge of most of the actual work and construction took place when he was the head of the project. The exact point at which his artistic freedom gave way to management responsibilities is difficult to specify and is a matter of controversy. A whole historical school of thought has questioned Herrera's leading role throughout the design process while recognising his technical and managerial input. Indeed, it is not easy to separate the two as his innovations were used as a means of reducing costs.

The most extreme viewpoint is currently that of Bury who echoed Portables in asserting that the myth of Herrera as the revolutionary architect of El Escorial was created in the mid-eighteenth century in order to establish the intellectual nature of the profession historically and nationally. Despite understating Herrera's role, Bury, almost by default, recognises his involvement in some of the most prominent adjustments or modifications to the project, the inspiration for which may have come from the

The dome of the Basilica from
the Clock Tower or Bell Tower.

king himself. Thus, even from this hostile standpoint, Herrera is credited with converting the enthusiastic King's sketches into architecture.

But ultimately this is tantamount to recognising Herrera's central role with regard to the co-ordination and therefore the supervision of the design, a position which he earned through sheer effort between 1569 and 1572. As Wilkinson-Zerner points out, the uniformity of El Escorial, totally free of inconsistency or inappropriate contrasts, indicates a sole designer or at least a leading one. Indeed, the building does not exemplify the variety of styles and methods that should have resulted from such diverse contributions. These contributions merge into an overall image whose rigour cannot be explained without the presence of an overall decision-maker who could only have been one architect, however much the king influenced him.

Indeed, Herrera's room for manoeuvre was as limited as his inventive powers. Despite his 'appropriation' of Juan Bautista de Toledo's work, Herrera constantly and implicitly recognised his own shortcomings and indebtedness. His name can be seen on only one of the drawings of El Escorial that he prepared for the prints by Perret, dated 1589: the tabernacle for the High Altar. According to Wilkinson-Zerner, this fact suggests that this was the only design that was entirely his own, without any trace of his predecessor.

The ambivalence of the King, who in 1582 agreed to call him "our architect" without granting him the appropriate salary until five years later, contributes to a climate of uncertainty countered by evidence that he was responsible for certain sections of the building.

The confusion is accentuated by the numerous consultations involving other Spanish and Italian architects carried out in the most diverse ways, ranging from individual to corporate reports and from contests to the redrafting of ideas. The depersonalization of creative endeavour reached a peak in the treatment and recycling of this mass of indigestible information. For some years after 1567, the construction process took on an international dimension with the request made to the Florence Academy for plans for the still uncertain basilica. Oddly, the

The Courtyard of the Evangelists from the windows of the Main Lower Cloister.

East Façade: the Ladies' Tower from
the terraces of the private gardens.

The Courtyard of the Masks in the centre of the King's House.

basilica would not be built following Vignola's synthetic designs but by following alternative plans presented by the modest Paciotto in 1562-63, who was in turn heavily influenced by the Herreresque modifications. As with the building's decorative painting, the appeal to Italy did not always result in total appreciation of the advice received.

In addition, we should not forget the contributions made by skilled craftsmen and master builders like friar Antonio de Villacastín, Pedro de Tolosa, Diego de Alcántara or Juan de Minjares, or those of the architects Gaspar de Vega and Francisco de Mora. The latter was a follower of Herrera and who continued his work from 1583 onwards. These names were associated with the propagation of the 'Herreresque' style and demonstrate the extent to which El Escorial had become an 'academy' or centre for artistic instruction from which suitably encoded new spatial concepts were transmitted.

Due to its own organizational system, the monastery was based on the work of a team whose final decisions relied on Philip II himself. The King not only supervised the construction personally but also had immediate control over the architect, both in terms of the appointment and the craftsmanship. Aside from this upper level of decision-making, the prior exercised the highest authority over the project. Below him, the "Congregation" was a practical committee with control over judicial and financial matters as well as inspections and payments. Overall, this was a cumulative project in which more emphasis seemed to be placed on the personal preferences of the King, albeit a brilliant amateur architectural enthusiast, than on the resourcefulness of the technical director of construction.

No less complicated is the monastery's "stylistic affiliation" to retain the terminology that has been used in attempts to categorize it. The terms referred to are on occasions merely descriptive or insignificant. Thus, reference has been made to an "unadorned", "simple" or "austere" style. This type of obvious categorisation became more analytically significant when Kubler pointed out that the "unadorned" style had previously appeared in Portugal – so closely associated with Philip II - as the simple (*chao*) style. The observation was not taken to its logical conclusion and remained no more than the suggestion of a possible connection. Camón Aznar also took a significant step by opting for a so-called "Trentine" style after considering the options of the terms "Escorial" and "Philippine" but his final, ideological-religious proposal, lacked the necessary specificity.

Clearer in this regard but not as a result any more acceptable, the ready appeal to a Mannerist style can only be considered in the generic sense of breaking the rules. Strictly speaking, Mannerism not only corresponds to a previous period but also to a different type of compositional or expressive freedom. Recent reappraisals tend to minimise its impact in Spain as an incoherent and superficial vehicle of vocabulary rather than a complete artistic language. Of course, El Escorial shows evidence of this range of formulae that had already become diluted in court architectural circles.

JUAN DE HERRERA
The Tempietto of
the Evangelists.

In order to give stylistic substance to the absence of adornment, Kubler turned away from the Portuguese idea and saw the monastery as an expression of the plainness of military design characteristic of military engineers such as Toledo and Paciotto. However, as Bury responded, the contribution of the latter was limited to the basilica whereas the former hardly gained recognition for work of this type. In addition, Bury reminds us that in the sixteenth century, "the principles of military architecture were founded on a very dif-

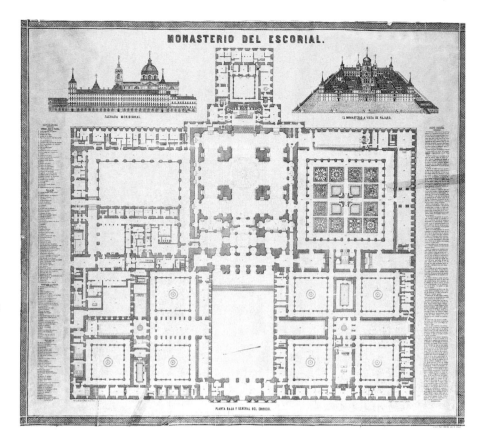

PEDRO SALCEDO DE LAS HERAS
General plan of the ground
floor of the Monastery of
El Escorial, 1876.
Lithograph.
Archivo General de Palacio.
Madrid.

ferent set of priorities from those in civil architecture" although there was no demarcation between these respective professional fields.

Bury even questions or places a relative value on the lack of adornment as a characteristic of the building, many of whose spaces are anti-Herreresque or not particularly austere. The Four Evangelist and Masks courtyards or the Sun Corridors as well as the interior decoration are indeed very different from this traditional image of severity.

From a more confident historical viewpoint, it can be stated that the monastery not only displayed the King and Toledo's preferences for the Serlian version of classicism but also the establishment of an exclusively Vitruvian style of architecture. The team working on El Escorial took from Vitruvius the dictates of symmetry, proportional unity and harmony. However, according to Marías and Bustamante, this is closer to a return to an interpretation of antiquity rather than of the Renaissance codification of such ideas.

The design owes a great deal to the simplified Italian Counter-Reformation architecture of the end of the 16th century. On the other hand, un-

Detail of the transept and the lateral
nave on the Epistle side. The Basilica.

executed designs such as the one for the 'Palladian' main façade indicate a controversial influence that does not seem to be sufficiently borne out in certain aspects of the basilica. In any case, there are a range of Italian borrowings in El Escorial, some more direct, others less so. Although the synthesis itself did not originate in Italy, the necessary material to create it came from there. This, in turn, served as the basis for another synthesis combining late Renaissance design with the Flemish tradition.

In the monastery, this successful Italian-Northern European synthesis, so close to the heart of Philip II, takes on unprecedented conceptual dimensions due to the huge scale and the rigour that accentuate Italian Counter-Reformation severity. Evidently, Philip II exercised greater influence over the design of El Escorial than, for example, Louis XIV in the case of Versailles.

Closely linked to the debate on style was the argument about the nature or effectiveness of some of the most important solutions derived from Italy by the El Escorial team. The result of this controversy is to set Herrera's critics against those who interpret his artistic licence as originality.

Courtyard and spire of the College.

While steering responsibility for the design towards the king, since Herrera is seen as a mere instrument of the monarch's architectural whims, John Bury stresses the very serious errors of implementation. Writing on the frontispiece of the main façade of the building, Bury says: "One is left bemused attempting to guess who might have been responsible for that surprising display of 'textbook architecture', a page torn out of Serlio" by an amateur, incompatible with the professionalism of Juan Bautista de Toledo.

As in the case of the style and the identity of the designer, the symbolism of the building gives rise to a debate that now veers between the esoteric to the exoteric. El Escorial can be read through Saint Augustine from the standpoint of Platonic idealism. Going beyond this, Taylor used a hermeneutic symbolism to interpret not only the architecture but also certain decorative features. Encumbered by this experimental approach, his mystical vision of El Escorial, hinging on Herrera's supposed occult personality via Lullism, has succeeded only in attracting the almost unanimous disapproval of researchers. By contrast, the political and religious significance of the monastery as the new Temple of Jerusalem has not been questioned although the date and the extent are a matter of debate. The theory, on the one hand, that Philip II deliberately imitated Solomon from a late stage in the construction process onwards and the supposition, on the other hand, that these aims originated with the monastery-palace, not only involve a different chronological interpretation but also a different perception of the ideological inspiration for the building.

The symbolic function combines with the architectural and practical ones in the context of the ground plan. The complexity of the plan arose not only from the juxtaposition of very diverse functions but also from the aim of integrating them into a precise unit expressing their common purpose as well as their hierarchy. Toledo's 'universal design', involving a system of courtyards, unmistakably proclaims the essential character of the whole building, presided over by a church. This design has been linked with the cruciform shapes of the hospitals of the Catholic Monarchs, buildings which also reveal Italian influence, but it has also been interpreted as a skilful reproduction of the layout of a medieval monastery.

Based on the axis formed by the main façade and a wing of the Library, the Kings' Courtyard, the Basilica and the Royal House, the property spreads out in two complementary symmetrical parts, on one side as a monastery and on the other as a school and a public or administrative palace. Each of these lateral extensions consists of an initial unit of four small courtyards in the shape of a cross with spacious cloisters behind. Not counting the Church and the library, the actual monastery itself covers as large an area as both the public palace and the school together. The former consists of its corresponding cruciform plan while the latter takes up the rest, i.e. the main courtyard.

Few ground-plans convey their ideological message with such effectiveness as that of the El Escorial foundation which is a truly expressive piece of architecture. It comprises the great central structure providing the backbone of the building with its two consecutive monumental façades, the repository of knowledge and the church with the pantheon underneath. At the end of a labyrinthine route, we come to the contradictory and deliberately modest king's residence which reflects the political and religious values of the Catholic Monarchy in the most readily identifiable terms, specifically in terms of Philip II's ideological vision.

The external façades

MICHEL-ANGE HOUASSE
View of El Escorial from the East, c.1720.
Patrimonio Nacional. Palace of La Moncloa.

The main entrance on the West Façade.

Above all a monastery, the whole building is situated on a particularly harsh and barren plain, emphasising its function as a retreat. However, various unmodifiable factors made it necessary to re move some auxiliary services from an already completed 'picture'. A decisive factor in this decision was the unsuitability of the holy royal site for menial manual duties. Thus, at the end of the construction process, the main block in the 'overall design' was flanked by three other buildings – The Compaña by Francisco de Mora and the two buildings known as the Casas de Oficio housing the staff quarters, attributed to Herrera.

The Casas de Oficio are inside La Lonja, an area extending along the main western façade of the monastery and also the northern one, under the shadow of the mountain. The gardens are arranged in a terrace on a heavy basement structure on the eastern and southern fringes and open out onto a descending landscape, their huge mass levelling out the uneven terrain. Orientated towards all four cardinal points, the altar facing east in accordance with canonical law, El Escorial turns ascetically away from tamed nature to confront the untamed country-

View of the northern and main or West façades from La Lonja.

East Façade.

The Tower and the Prior's Garden, and the King's private gardens seen from the rooms of the King's Quarter.

side. But the borders of the gardens with the King's House, a kind of semi-independent traditional villa, and the aptly named "Sun Corridors" prove that the rigorous spirit of the foundation did not prevent a humanistic counterbalance which is as important for an understanding of the monastery as the clinical 'Herreresque' stereotype.

    The centripetal force of the whole ensemble manifests its intentions. The impression of uniformity would not have been so overwhelming if Toledo's original idea had been put into practice, namely to lower the height of the western section and to have towers in the middle of the flanks in order to provide a smooth transition where the two levels join. The doubling of the number of monks, a measure introduced in 1564, resulted in this saturation or interruption of this smooth progression. Although accentuating the impression of vastness, it was detrimental to achieving proportional harmony.

    Following Toledo's *universal design,* the whole building occupies a rectangular space of 207 m by 162 m. The outstanding feature is the King's

The Monastery from the Forge Meadow from the south-east.

The spire of one of the
Monastery's towers seen
from the trees around the
building.

The Lantern Patio, between
the four smaller cloisters of
the Monastery.

House, the handle, as it were, of the legendary grille used in the martyrdom of Saint Lawrence, thus explaining the complex ground plan. No construction of the time came anywhere near these dimensions. Nor, as a result, could they match the many other statistics of this "eighth wonder". The colossal scale of the monument is illustrated by sixteen courtyards, fifteen cloisters, eighty-six staircases, nine towers, eighty-eight fountains, one thousand two hundred doors and two thousand six hundred windows (two hundred and sixty-six in the main façade alone).

The dome of the basilica reaches a height of 92 m while the bell towers are 72 m high and the angular towers 45 m high. Once the middle towers in Toledo's plan had been abandoned, these gave El Escorial the appearance of a Spanish fortress. Enclosed within a wide area by these four boundary markers, the monastery is characterized by an enveloping uniformity. At first sight, the only distinctive features are the entranceways on the main façade, the Royal House and the Sun Corridors, individual architectural elements that only serve to highlight the hermetic atmosphere pervading the whole building.

The exotic roof in the Flemish style, already tried out by Philip II at El Pardo and Valsaín, introduces a degree of distortion in the style that does not affect its overall fixed image. Nevertheless, it does not weaken but, instead, reinforces the overall cohesion of the external features. In 1568, the King asked Juan de Herrera to draw up a small-scale model for the roofing, which had already been the subject of some designs by Gaspar de Vega. Following the fire in 1671, Bartolomé Zumbigo replaced them and changed the design of the lanterns and the spires. These regained their original Herreresque form, as shown in the prints by Perret, when the wooden structure was replaced by a different metal one in the 1560s.

Beneath the apparent uniformity of façades in which an economy of expression allows the patterning of the walls to be dictated by the repeated ranges of windows, there is a subtle underlying range of techniques. Of course, the main façade is an exception to this much-maligned uniformity. Three entrances are superimposed against the vast backdrop of this façade. The side entrances are identical and correspond to the school (to the left of the observer) and to the monastery. The latter is simply a tradesman's entrance leading to the monastery area with access to the food stores by means of a ramp. Beyond, we can see first the impressive kitchen and

The East Façade.
Detail of the exterior of the Basilica, the King's House
and the Palace from the Palace Garden.

then the splendid light, a covered courtyard between the four smaller cloisters. The school has a similar layout (also closed to the public). Here, the outstanding feature is the assembly hall or "theatre" to use its original term.

The central entrance leads into the basilica through the Kings' Courtyard and is therefore the main one of the monastery. Following the duplication in the number of monks in 1564, with the consequent increased height of the western section of the building, Juan Bautista de Toledo contributed new ideas for this façade. According to Bustamente García, between 1573 and 1574, when designs already existed, the problem of its definitive appearance was tackled, including the incorporation of the library. Use was made of the traditional Spanish solution of positioning it above the entrance, a method first proposed at the Santa Cruz college in Valladolid. Herrera located the library complex over the façade like a great prismatic block substituting the two towers in Toledo's initial plan.

However, the result is not and could not be a university façade with an upper section recognisable as a library. The frontispiece does not indicate this function although it is supported by the library structure. Instead, it alludes to the basilica in a vaguely symbolic religious sense lacking in actual substance. As Bury pointed out, a façade of a church has been taken from Serlio but it has been reproduced "out of context" and perversely. Serlio proposed a church with three naves but here the façade has been imposed on the building without any structural consistency and without taking into account the purpose of the building. Bury suggested that Philip II himself was the designer although responsibility for the implementation of the building plans lay with Herrera.

The royal coat of arms and a large statue of Saint Lawrence add interest to the enormous decorations on the column in the central part of the upper section. The statue is 4 metres high and is made of granite although the head and hands are in marble. It was commissioned from Juan Bautista Monegro in 1582 who also designed the coat of arms.

The picturesque eastern or rear façade where the graceful staircase of the King's House maintains an uneasy dialogue with the cold wall

The South Façade.
The Monks' Garden from the east gallery of the Convalescents' Gallery or Sun Galleries.

of the church, is in contrast to the sobriety of the lateral façades. The north-ern one includes an almost unnoticeable contribution by the Neo-classical architect Juan de Villanueva. In 1793, Villanueva had to decide on a new access to the building now known as the Public or Administrative Palace.

At one end of the southern façade, the convalescent's Gallery for sick monks opens out into two sections, functioning as a huge containing wall which evens out the differences in height between the garden and La Lonja. The evident Italianate style of these Sun Corridros did not prevent Íñiguez from attributing the gallery to Herrera, to the detriment of Toledo, and putting the date to 1574. As Javier Ribera demonstrated, in an idea al-ready been anticipated by Zuazo, the project was undoubtedly designed by Juan Bautista. Begun in 1564 and interrupted three years later, the resump-tion of the project in 1574 entailed transferring the credit for the design to a man who, at least in this case, was merely its executor.

The South Façade.
The Dispensary, the
Convalescents' Gallery and
the Monastery from the
Garden Pond.

The Basilica

FRAY JULIÁN DE LA FUENTE DEL SAZ
The Annunciation. Choirbook n. 167.
Illuminated manuscript, parchment,
16th-century.
Ante-choir of the Basilica.

The Façade of the Basilica.
The Patio of the Kings.

Crossing the entrance vestibule, under the library block, the visitor enters the Kings' Courtyard (*Patio de Reyes*), designed with lateral porticoes by Juan Bautista de Toledo but subsequently greatly simplified as a neutral background to the impressive façade of the basilica.

The particular characteristics of the church project are almost as unfathomable as the nature of the construction process. Not only is the ground plan by Juan Bautista de Toledo unknown but, in addition, the theories posited by Javier Ribera cover a range of different possibilities although they all include one element in common; a semicircular structure between two towers. With the apse as a starting-point, a space was marked out for the church within the overall scheme prior to 1563. This allowed for a wide range of combinations. In 1562, the intervention of Francesco Paciotto, who favoured a flat end wall, saw the beginning of a very confused period of modifications and reconsiderations. The situation did not become clear until 1575 when work began over the foundations. The ground was levelled out in 1572 but two years later the King was still hesitating between the alternatives offered by Toledo and Paciotto.

It seems that in 1562-63 when Paciotto presented his design, consultations took place with his compatriots involving a parallel request for new plans. In 1567, a number of designs were sent to the Florence Academy for a decision to be made one way or another. Following another request for artistic assistance made by the Spanish Court to the Academy in 1571, the former gave fresh impetus to the slow process in 1572 by appointing a panel to produce a synthesis which would be submitted to the superior judgement of Vignola.

In 1573, a verdict from this very prolonged and laborious process reached royal circles but the contents of this report are unknown. At this point, Herrera devoted himself in full to studying this complex issue. The King rejected the contributions from Florence and Rome, stating that they were not of any great benefit. This gave Herrera responsibility for solving a problem that could not be put off any longer. In the opinion of Bustamante García, the monarch's refusal to accept the Italian work was a judgement based not on merit but on practicalities, taking into account that what Herrera was offering by 1573 was an elevation of the church (with the idea of the apse definitely ruled out).

Finally, at a decisive moment in 1574, Philip II ruled in favour of Paciotto in accordance with a final reassessment by Herrera, whose syncretic project started to take shape the following year. Vignola, having seen his project rejected, apparently declined an invitation to visit Spain. However, questions remain for the presence of so many important Italian references in the design of the church.

The issue of Palladian influence is a matter of controversy, supported by Kubler but rejected by Bustamente García. According to the latter, although Paciotto was responsible for the idea of a square church with displaced towers, Juan Bautista de Toledo should be attributed with the evident similarity of the basilica to St Peter's in Rome. In this sense, the building reflects the combination of a centralized structure with a longitudinal layout proposed by the architect Giuliano Sangallo the Younger. Moreover, the link with the Vatican would reach Bramante through Michelangelo who was, as we should bear in mind, Juan Bautista's master. It can therefore be said that Herrera's design, although deriving from contemporary Italian work and tending towards a reassessment of Vitruvian classical architecture, nevertheless contained many elements characteristic of his predecessor Toledo.

The church clearly evinces Herrera's undoubted talents for organization, a task in which he was assisted by Friar Antonio de Villacastín,

ANONYMOUS ITALIAN

Saint Lawrence.

Marble and gilt-bronze, 16th-century.

Choir of the Basilica.

Panoramic View of the West of the building from Mount Abantos: The Basilica presides over the Royal Library and the roofs of the Monastery.

but also his equally conspicuous skill at drawing up and redesigning the plans of others, guided by the King's erratic instructions.

The extraordinary, albeit controversial and indeed incoherent main façade has two storeys. The lower part is articulated by two powerful Doric columns which become two large statues on pedestals on the upper storey, itself without an order.

Separated from this central structure by two small axes formed by the fronts of the side aisles, the towers, with a height of 72 m, are situated between the perpendicular wings of the courtyard, creating a strangely disjointed effect. The one on the right of the observer is the clock-tower or bell-tower while the one on the left is for small bells, in honour of a set of Flemish bells reinstalled in 1988.

Within the complicated process of constructing the church, the façade, by default, must be attributed to Herrera, who developed Toledo and Paciotto's unclear proposals. According to Kubler, Palladian influence is evident in the narthex-lower choir ensemble, in the linking of the portico with

The Courtyard of the Kings from
the windows of the Royal Library.

Sculptures of the Kings of the House of Judah on the
cornice of the entablature on the façade of the Basilica.
Courtyard of the Kings.

the tetrastyle hall located at the entrance, in the manner of a true "basilica". The upper section of this façade as well as the transept façades are characterized by the Syrian pediment, whose tympanum is penetrated by the semicircular which arch breaks the entablature. Although this motif is perhaps unorthodox, it was used in Italian Renaissance architecture.

The façade disconcerted Bury, who did not believe that it could have been designed by Herrera. He therefore returned to the idea of a possible personal initiative by Philip II, once again with the technical assistance of his favourite exponent.

The disturbing impression of incoherence between the two storeys is increased in the upper level by the replacement of the intended obelisks with statues which, although large, lack structural coherence and the upper level lacks a defined architectural style. The Hebrew scholar Arias Montano proposed the idea of placing the six kings of Judah there, thus making the connection with the design of the temple of Jerusalem and emphasising the Salomonic vocation of the monastery. Commissioned from Juan Bautista Monegro in 1580, the granite and marble sculptures have gilt-bronze attributes by Sebastián Fernández. The stone for the six kings and for the figure of Saint Lawrence was extracted from a single block in a quarry in the nearby mountains. A commemorative inscription was etched on this block: "seis reyes y un santo / salieron de este canto / y quedó para otro tanto" (six kings and a saint / came out of this quarry / and there is still stone for as many more). Although popular accounts have stated the weight of the stone monarchs to be around 20,000 kilos, in fact they do not weigh more than 6,000.

JUAN BAUTISTA MONEGRO and SEBASTIÁN FERNÁNDEZ *Jehoshaphat and Hezekiah, kings of the House of Judah* Granite, marble and gilt-bronze, 1580. Courtyard of the Kings.

The basilica is divided into two clearly differentiated but interconnected parts. Behind the façade, we can see the choir and the lower choir area. The latter, as its name indicates, is situated below the choir. Next come the royal chapel and the monastery church. The lower choir, serving as a holy area for the laity, is a small scale-reproduction of the much larger one in the form of a Greek cross reserved for the court and the monks or the main body of the church.

Main north organ and the lantern of the dome.

Nave of the transept of the Basilica

A daringly flat vault covers the central section, an exercise in virtuosity and decorative work and illustrates the technical capacity of Herrera's team. According to Bustamante García, the under-arch may derive from a design made by Juan Bautista de Toledo in about 1567, however, by 1562 both Paciotto and Toledo had worked on Madrid churches where this technique is apparent with the same tetrastyle layout. However, in the case of the convent of Las Descalzas Reales, where the design is still evident but drastically modified, the extent of their respective contributions is so unclear as to prevent us from drawing any definitive conclusions.

In the lower choir, two altars were used to say mass to the congregation on either side of the intervening arch leading to the royal monastery area. In front of this was a large bronze grille forged in Saragossa by Guillén de Tujarón and after this the small seminarists' choir.

The church, strictly speaking, is an imposing square with 50 m sides in the shape of a Greek cross with the addition Main which penetrates into the body of King's House. The church is completed by a dome which is 92 m high but quite narrow, as the slight bevelling of the central columns does not provide it with the necessary space to spring up. Even so, the powerful Doric pilasters create a vigorous and majestic interior, a truly original creation in the wider context of contemporary architecture.

The inclusion of thermal windows was not necessarily due to the influence of Palladio, as Kubler suggested, since they already belonged to a common architectural heritage,; the ingenuity of Herrera.

Within a frame of reference whose maximum exponent is St Peter's in Rome, the church of El Escorial is comparable to that of Saint Mary of Carignano in Genoa, a project commissioned from Galeazzo Alessi in 1549 who died in 1572 before its completion. A reworking of an original project by Bramante for the Vatican, Alessi's church differed from Herrera's in various ways including the excessively lavish architectural ornamentation, which could almost be described as vulgar according to Peter Murray, a criticism cannot by any measure be levelled at the church of El Escorial which found in Herrera the catalyst for the creation of the solemn and devout royal style favoured by Philip II.

The conjunction of the dome and the four vaults of the naves.
Transept of the Basilica.

JUAN DE HERRERA
Large Choirbook Stand.
Jasper, marble, gilt-bronze, wood and iron.
16th-century.
Choir of the Basilica.

In accordance with the guidelines already established in Spain for funerary areas, the main chapel is furnished with three distinctive elements – the altarpiece in the centre and, at right angles to this, the two cenotaphs, all in compliance with Juan de Herrera's classicising and canonical proposal. The main altarpiece is 26 metres high and 14 metres wide. It not only reinvigorated a type traditionally executed in wood by the use of high-quality materials, but it also reduced and simplified its brightly coloured compartmentalised structure, resulting in an architectural model that would remain in favour until well into the seventeenth century. Commissioned in 1579 with its figurative sculpture and tabernacle, it was clearly envisaged as a inter-linked structure with three sections and a top, and conforming to the logical hierarchy of the orders. Within this framework could be inserted the rigorous iconography which, in the eyes of its patron, a church required, particularly when that church was El Escorial.

The King's Oratory, beneath the cenotaph of Philip II. This connects the High Altar of the Basilica to the King's Chamber.

As on many other similar occasions, it was not for aesthetic reasons but, rather on account of expendiency or propriety that Philip II dispensed with what appeared to be the most suitable object to preside over the basilical altar: the great *Martrydom of Saint Lawrence* painted by Titian between 1564 and 1567 and still in the so-called Old or Borrowed Church. 1576 saw the death of Philip II's favourite painter, the one whom he would have liked to have entrusted with producing new works of art for the altarpiece. Titian's natural successor, Navarrete el Mudo died in 1579, the year in which the architecture and the sculptures were commissioned.

Tintoretto and Veronese both sent canvases but although their paintings, and Titian's were highly regarded by the monarch, they were considered to be unsuitable for El Escorial. In another development, both Tintoretto and Veronese, leading artists of the Venetian school, refused to come to Spain to work *in situ*. If we also bear in mind that Tintoretto and Veronese's contributions are not now generally considered autograph, the attitude of these two painters seems to be one of disappointing indifference.

Finally, in 1586, Federico Zuccaro, the most distinguished of the Italian painters who answered the call from El Escorial, took charge of producing eight canvases for the main altarpiece. However, in addition to finishing touches there were also changes, as the hard-to-please monarch

Basilica. High Altar (1579-88), designed by JUAN DE HERRERA.

Marble sculpture carved by JACOME DA TREZZO and GIOVAN BATTISTA COMANE.

Bronze sculptures by LEONE and POMPEO LEONI.

Paintings by PELLEGRINO TIBALDI and FEDERICO ZUCCARO.

JUAN DE HERRERA

Tabernacle, made by JACOME DA TREZZO.

Coloured marbles, jaspers and gilt-bronze, 1579-86.

High Altar of the Basilica.

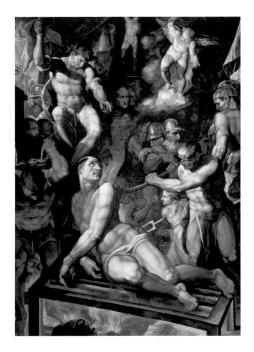

was dissatisfied with him. Three of Zuccaro's paintings had to make way for others by Pellegrino Tibaldi who produced an *Adoration of the Shepherds* and *Adoration of the Magi* on either side of the tabernacle in the first section, while in the central passage of the second section is his *Martyrdom of Saint Lawrence*. On either side of this painting are works by Zuccaro: *The Flagellation* and *Christ carrying the Cross*. Zuccaro's work in the third section consists of *The Ascension of Christ* and *The Descent of The Holy Spirit*.

All of the sculpture is in gilt bronze and was produced in the Milan workshop of Leone and Pompeo Leoni. Initially, the work was intended to be partly polychrome, but the unifying effect of gold overrode Spanish preferences. The two superimposed recesses on each of the far inter-columnal spaces have sculptures of The Fathers of the Church in the first section and The Four Evangelists in the second. Saint James and Saint Andrew are on either side of the third section. On the top, we can see Saint Peter and Saint Paul. Also on the upper level is a Calvary with Christ on the cross between the Virgin and Saint John, a grouping traditionally ascribed to Pompeo, whereas the rest of the work would have been carried out by his father.

In spite of the obvious differences in quality to be found in these refined examples of courtly art produced by the Leoni, it is difficult to be precise about authorship. According to Mulcahy, the contribution of the son, assisted in turn by the Flemish sculptor Adriaen de Vries, is more significant.

FEDERICO ZUCCARO

(Left)

The Flagellation.

(Right)

Christ bearing the Cross.

PELLEGRINO TIBALDI

(Centre)

The Martyrdom of Saint Lawrence.

Second level of the altarpiece.

High Altar of the Basilica.

In the lower section is the beautiful tabernacle created between 1579 and 1586 by Jacopo da Trezzo using different varieties of Spanish marble and based on designs by Juan de Herrera. A brilliant technical exercise, it is even more interesting as an archetype which expresses the most sophisticated uses of space in the late Renaissance. The structure of this circular shrine is reinforced by Corinthian columns in blood-red jasper which was so hard that Trezzo had to invent special tools in order to turn it on a lathe. The columns support a double entablature topped by a dome with a lantern. The interior housed the custodium or monstrance of similar composition, one of the many treasures that disappeared during the French invasion.

Behind the altarpiece, we can see the Sacrarium or *camarín,* a small chapel painted in fresco by Pellegrino Tibaldi. It anticipates a use of space characteristic of Spanish architecture, which fully express itself in the Baroque period.

The cenotaphs are characteristic of Herrera's work, expressing architectural grandeur and simplicity in equal measure. The concept is closely linked to the structure of the main altar. Their high plinths include small chapels or oratories adjoining the royal bedrooms. Following the arrangement of the Emperor's room at Yuste, these chapels enabled the royal observers to follow the ceremonies on the high altar obliquely and discreetly from the privacy of their apartments. Above, a tribunal takes the form of a gallery with a screen of Doric columns, and houses a group of funerary sculptures of the royal figures. The upper level displays the respective royal coats of arms.

On the Gospel side on the right as seen from the altar is the figure of Charles V, armed and wearing an imperial robe. The Emperor is accompanied by his wife Isabel, the mother of Philip II, also in the foreground and behind a shared prie-dieu. Behind the Emperor is his daughter Mary, the empress of Germany, kneeling like her parents. Finally, the standing figures are Charles V's sisters Mary of Hungary and Eleanor of France.

Similarly, the monument opposite is a tribute in death to the founder whose figure appears in the foreground together with his fourth wife, Ann of Austria. Behind the King, we see the figure of his third wife, Isabel de Valois, also kneeling. The two other standing figures are Maria of Portugal and the ill-fated prince Carlos.

The Leoni workshop was entrusted to produce both groups of figures as well as the sculpture on the high altar. In fact, the workshop now

Juan de Herrera

Cenotaph of Philip II, 1592-1600, above the King's Oratory.

Epistle side. Main Chapel of the Basilica.

Jacome da Trezzo "el Mozo", G.P. Cambiago and G. Miseroni:

coloured marbles, jaspers and hardstones.

Pompeo Leoni: bronzes.

POMPEO LEONI

Cenotaph of Charles V, c. 1592-1597, detail.

Gilt-bronze, hardstones, jaspers and coloured marbles.

Evangelist side, Main Chapel of the Basilica.

The Emperor; his wife, the Empress Elizabeth of Portugal;

his daughter Maria, Empress of Germany; his sisters, Maria,

Queen of Hungary and Leonora, Queen of France.

EXTRVXIT SIBI VIVENS P.

QVIESCVNT SIMVL ANNA
ELISABETHA ET MARIA VXO...
CVM CAROLO PRINC.FIL.PRIN...

Pompeo Leoni

Cenotaph of Philip II, 1592-1600, detail.

Gilt-bronze, hardstones, jaspers and coloured marbles.

Epistle side. Main Chapel of the Basilica.

The King; his niece and fourth wife, Anne of Austria, mother
of Philip III; his third wife Isabel de Valois; his first wife,
Maria of Portugal and their son, Prince Carlos.

The King's coat-of-arms, detail of the Ionic attic level.

Gilt-bronze, hardstones, jaspers and coloured marbles.

Reliquary in the form of
Milan Cathedral, opened out.
Blued and damascened iron.
Milan, 16th-century.
Reliquary of Saint Jerome.
Epistle side of the Basilica.

only consisted of Pompeo who had moved to Madrid. The production
process lasted from 1592, the date when the first contract was signed, until
1600. It involved numerous instances of trial and error, alterations etc., again
revealing the difficulties in developing a new image for the monarchy. Polychrome marble was the first idea for the figures and the use of gilding therefore conformed to the decision for the main altar. The unifying effect of the
gilding meant that all the sculpture merged to create an overall impression
of splendour and magnificence.

In the meantime, the august portraits were completed rather slowly
as the family group of Charles V was not installed until 1598 and that of
Philip II not until two years later when the sovereign had already been dead
for two years. While the portraits were being prepared, plaster substitutes
were used instead, an ephemeral or provisional decoration whose appearance
is recorded in a number of interesting paintings preserved in the building.

Pompeo's skills, with an approach approximating that of the decorative arts, are evident in his use of a detachable cloak, a device already
used by Leone Leoni for the armour of *Charles V and the Fury*. It is also

BENVENUTO CELLINI

Crucified Christ, c. 1559-62. Carrara marble.

Chapel of the Doctors. Basilica.

Benvenuto Cellini
Crucified Christ, c. 1559-62 (detail).

evident in the virtuosity of the inlaid hardstone coat of arms covering the robe and it is no coincidence that the silversmith Juan de Arfe assisted in the casting of the royal group.

According to Von der Osten Sacken, the worshipping figures become absorbed into the formal and conceptual uniformity of the chancel due to the "factor of perpetual adoration", present in Spain since the end of the fifteenth century. In anticipation of Charles V's final wishes, eucharistic exaltation determined the position and the pose of the statues. As Mulcahy put it, "these are the most impressive royal fu-neral monuments in the whole of European art." Philip II's inner sanctuary in his palace-monastery seems to be revealed by a no less Spanish Baroque dramatic effect. The founder virtually slept on his grave and prayed beneath the spot destined to hold his own sepulchral ef-figy at prayer.

The basilica contains forty-two paint-ed altarpieces. The two largest are located at the end of the side aisles. These are reliquary altars dedicated to the *Annunciation and to Saint Jerome in the Desert* commissioned from Federico Zuc-caro in 1586-88. Zuccaro proved to be the greatest failure at El Escorial and the obscure Spaniard Juan Gómez who worked in the service of the King as a supervisor of paintings, particularly with regard to the iconographic components, was particularly merciless with these composi-tions. Philip II was obsessed with collecting relics as an assertion of Catholicism against Protestant heresy, initiating a veritable museum of them eventually numbering around 7,500.

The remaining altarpieces were distributed among the chapels and recesses of the Basilica. The five next largest were painted between 1584 and 1592. Two of them have canvases by Luca Cambiaso and another two are decorated with paintings by Pellegrino Tibaldi. The last altarpiece in this sequence is *The Martyrdom of Saint Maurice and the Theban Legion* painted by Romolo Cinciannato in 1584 to replace the version by El Greco. According to Mulcahy, "it is a perfect example of late Mannerism, a piece of clinical virtuosity in which the most outstanding aspects are the elegant postures and musculature reminiscent of Michelangelo."

LUCA GIORDANO
The Glorification of the Immaculate Conception,
c. 1692-94.
Fresco of the south-west vault at the end of the Epistle nave. Basilica.

The Israelites crossing the
Red Sea, c. 1692-94.
Fresco on the vault.
Northern arm of the
transept nave. Basilica.

The final group is formed by thirty-three smaller altarpieces with
canvases painted by several Spanish artists between 1576 and 1584. These
were Juan Fernández de Navarrete *el Mudo*, Alonso Sánchez Coello, Luis
de Carvajal and Diego de Urbina. All except one of these canvas paintings
depict pairs of saints. According to Mulcahy, the series has the iconographic coherence and consistency demanded by Philip II.

In one of the lower chapels is a splendid example of Italian Renaissance sculpture: the superb *Crucified Christ* carved in Carrara marble by
Benvenuto Cellini between 1559 and 1562. It was intended to be placed on
the sculptor's own tomb in the Florentine church of La Santissima Annun-
ziata. An entirely personal creation, signed and dated 1562 on the lower
section, the concept and the technique are indebted to Michelangelo's aesthetic. Duke Francisco I de' Medici, whose father bought the sculpture
from Cellini, eventually presented it as a gift to Philip II in 1576.

Around 1830, Ferdinand VII commissioned Manuel de Urquiza
to produce the two pulpits, while two great bronze candelabra complete
the furnishing of the Basilica.

Only the frescoes in the choir and on the dome of the chancel date from the earliest phase of the building's foundation. The rather clinically correct chancel was created in about 1584 by Luca Cambiaso, known in Spain as Luqueto. It represents *The Trinity* or the *Coronation of the Virgin* with Mary as the central protagonist, a concession to the Madrid court that the Genoese would not have allowed himself in his home country.

In sharp contrast to the academic nature of Cambiaso's work and also to the architecture of the church, are the spectacular and highly Baroque frescoes on another eight vaults produced by Luca Giordano between 1693 and 1694. Moreover, Giordano tried to encourage Cambiaso to repaint his contribution in accordance with his own ornate style. In Giordano (known in Spain as Lucas Jordán) Charles II saw the brilliant and above all fast interior designer that he needed to carry out a great programme of decoration not only in the basilica but also for the main staircase of the monastery.

The speed with which, at the age of almost sixty, Giordano met these objectives, completing the work in twenty-two months between September 1692 and July 1964, justified his nickname of 'Fa presto'. But Charles II was not Philip II. Nor was Giordano willing to relinquish the modern status of the artist. The subject matter was decided not only by the King but also by the monks and the painter himself, who clashed with the sovereign over his iconographic convictions.

Over the main section of the lower choir, the central nave extends towards the façade with no other architectural articulation than the cornice of the entablature. This space is 27 m long, 14 m wide and 23 m high. It forms the monks' choir. Enrique Cotén carved the woodwork of the organs and José Flecha the one hundred and twenty-four choir-stalls. One of these, in the south-east corner, is slightly more spacious. This was the one used by Philip II who followed the religious services like an other nameless monk.

Between 1584 and 1585, Luca Cambiaso painted the vast and often criticised fresco on the dome variously entitled *The Adoration of the Trinity, The Glory* or *The Paradise*. This is complemented by a painting on the far wall of *The Annunciation*.

The Monks' Choir.
JUAN DE HERRERA
Choirstalls by
Giuseppe Flecha

D. O. M.

LOCVS SACER MORTALITATIS EXVVIIS
CATHOLICORVM REGVM
A RESTAVRATORE VITÆ CVIVS ARÆ MAXIMÆ
AVSTRIACA ADHVC PIETATE SVBIACENT
OPTATAM DIEM EXPECTANTIVM.

QVAM POSTHVMAM SEDEM SIBI ET SVIS
CAROLVS CÆSARVM MAX. INVOTIS HABVIT.
PHILIPPVS II. REGVM PRVDENTISS. ELEGIT.
PHILIPPVS III. VERE PIVS INCHOAVIT.

PHILIPPVS IIII.
CLEMENTIA CONSTANTIA RELIGIONE MAGNVS
AVXIT ORNAVIT ABSOLVIT
ANN. DOM. M. DC. LIIII.

NATVRA OCCIDIT.

EXALTAT SPES.

The Pantheons

GIOVANNI ANTONIO CERONI
One of the wall-lights with
candle-bearing angels by
Giovanni de Monaco. Gilt-bronze.
Pantheon of Kings.

GIOVANNI BATTISTA CRESCENZI
Door to the Pantheon of Kings with the coat-of-arms of
Philip IV flanked by allegories of the Decline of Nature
and the Exaltation of Hope, 1654.
Marble, gilt-bronze and enamel.

THE PANTHEON OF KINGS

The original and primary function of El Escorial
was to provide a burial place for Charles V and
also for Philip II, its founder. As a result of the
logical extension of this function, it began to as-
sume an initially dynastic and subsequently institutional role that has lasted with some exceptions,
to this day. Within this overall historical context,
the two pantheons correspond to very different
centuries and aesthetic approaches. Whereas the
Pantheon of Kings, dating from the seventeenth
century, is a remarkable example of Baroque architecture, the nineteenth-century Pantheon of
the Infantes (royal princes) is a prime example of
stylistic eclecticism.

Paradoxically, the founder was not able
to complete a functional burial area worthy of
the magnificence of the cenotaphs: a pantheon of
kings. According to some of his biographers,
Philip said that he had prepared a place to re-
ceive God and that his son, if he so wished,
would construct it in order to house his bones
and those of his parents. Kubler stated that when
Philip II died, El Escorial had been completed
with the exception of the structure that was the

basic and original purpose of the building, namely the circular underground burial chamber destined to hold the dynastic tombs. Built following designs by Juan de Herrera, the crypt, Kubler added, lacked decoration, illumination and drainage. Consequently, the royal remains were provisionally kept in another crypt located above the first one. This resulted in the body of Charles V lying under the priest who was taking the service.

As in so many other aspects of the obscure history of the building, serious doubts arise concerning the identity of the architect. According to Bustamante, when Juan Bautista de Toledo died in 1567, the pantheon and the surrounding area i.e. the intermediary crypt, had been completed in terms of layout and the general features and only the architectural articulation was lacking. Work on the pantheon was already underway: covered by a semi-circular dome without oculus, it had the same proportions as the legendary Roman building whose name it shared.

Whether the pantheon was the work of Toledo or whether it resulted from a reassessment by Herrera, it is always seen in the light of its main purpose by analysts studying the intentions of Philip II and his architects. Bearing in mind its eventual function, interpretations are based on the premise that this circular underground space was destined as a collective burial place. Bustamante even discerned certain spaces that could be intended to hold urns in an overall plan drawn up by Herrera but reused and altered in the seventeenth century. Thus, the intermediary underground chapel can be seen as a temporary pantheon compared with the definitive version which took the form of a chapel below the church. The completion of the dome was commissioned in 1569 and work started a year later.

Leaving aside speculation about the founder's beliefs regarding the supreme importance of the divine 'resting place', it is difficult to understand why Philip II curtailed plans to build a large circular crypt. According to Bustamante, financial difficulties at the beginning of his successor's reign led to the total interruption of work on the monastery. Consequently, the unfinished pantheon was temporarily forgotten. However, if work on the pantheon dome had started in 1570, the subsequent delay of thirty years cannot be explained.

Despite insufficient finances, Philip III decided to pursue the pantheon project to its conclusion which did not, however, come about until the end of the following reign. According to Kubler, from 1617 to 1635, Giovanni Battista Crescenzi transformed the circular design into an octagonal one but the project was thwarted once again and was not resumed until ten years later, this time by Friar Nicolás de Madrid who was assisted by Alonso

Altar of the Pantheon of Kings.

DOMENICO GUIDI: *Crucified Christ,* c. 1657. Gilt-bronze.

FRAY EUGENIO DE LA CRUZ and FRAY JUAN DE LA CONCEPCIÓN: altar frontal. Gilt-bronze.

JUAN GÓMEZ DE MORA,
GIOVANNI BATTISTA
CRESCENZI
Hemi-cycle with the
funerary urns of the
reigning kings and queens.
Coloured marbles, jaspers
and gilt-bronze.
Pantheon of Kings, 1617-54.

Carbonell and Bartolomé Zumbigo and completed work around 1654. According to Kubler's timescale, however, new designs had to be presented for the floor and the lunettes although these were based on the premise of using material assembled by Crescenzi, including both the marble and the bronze mounts, the latter commissioned from Italy in 1618-19 from his own designs.

According to Llaguno, Carbonell was responsible for the designs of the floor, the altar and the new entrance with the staircase. All of this work would have been actually carried out by Zumbigo.

The Supervisor of Royal Construction Projects, Giovanni Battista Crescenzi, would have had control over the decorative work, including the marble wall coverings and the bronze ornamentation. For this, he could count on the collaboration of Pedro de Lizargarate and Bartolomé Zumbigo the Elder respectively as well as the assistance of several Italian artists, above all from Genoa. However, the overall project must be attributed to Juan Gómez de Mora, although it took on a more decorative character under Philip IV.

This second phase saw the decoration of the dome, the stairways and their entrances. Also during this period the definitive tiled floor was put in place and new bronze decoration incorporated, in addition to the solution of serious technical problems. A contemporary observer, Friar Francisco de los Santos, implied that both Pedro de Lizargarate and Crescenzi himself contributed equally to the proposals. However, apart from his skills as a marble carver, Pedro de Lizargarate's involvement seems to have been limited to an attempt to lower the original level of the floor in order to accommodate the great Baroque installation. The chamber then flooded with water from a spring and Friar Nicolas de Madrid had to use his ingenuity to tackle the crisis and, in doing so, he by chance opened a window. Lighting and drainage thus ceased to be obstacles.

Passing from the church into the Sacristy, we see a bronze door with a Latin inscription of 1654. Behind this door, three flights of stairs covered in marble and jasper lead to the magnificent Pantheon of Kings. With its semicircular vault, the chamber is of a circular shape divided into eight sections.

Pairs of Corinthian columns provide the main pattern in the octagonal crypt. Between them are shelves of sarcophagi orientated towards the altar. The eight segments of the dome are perforated by corresponding lunettes. As Goya Nuño pointed out, the alternating use of marbles and bronze goes back to the earliest period of the building's history but with a contrasting aesthetic, ranging from the stylized grotesque decoration of the vault to the most elaborate and Baroque detail on the frieze and the corbels of the recesses, culminating in the decoration on the urns.

The rich combination of these materials, with different shades of marble – bluish from Toledo and reddish from Tortosa – the courtly pomp of the Corinthian order, the exuberance of the grotesques, and the well-arranged sculptural and supplementary elements, all make the pantheon an example of the early Baroque. The superstructure imposes itself on the original late-Renaissance aesthetic, as does the Italian or Italianate embellishment over the work by Gómez de Mora. In conclusion, the result is more international than Spanish.

Bernini's magnificent bronze *Christ,* measuring 140 cm high, presided over the altar until at least 1657. Today, it is kept in the College chapel, which is not open to visitors. As Wittkower stressed, it is the only surviving work that Bernini produced for the Spanish court. This was not the only crucifix to be removed on account of its excessive size. The one commissioned prior to 1635 from Pietro Tacca and measuring 190 cm suffered a similar fate. It is now in the side-chapel of the Sacristy.

The Funerary urns of the reigning kings and queens on the Evangelist side (to the left of the viewer) and those of the male and female consorts on the Epistle side (to the right). Pantheon of Kings.

Shortly after Bernini's crucifix was removed it was permanently replaced by a smaller one by Domenico Guidi. This was only 125 cm high, the smallest so far. The feet are pinned down by two nails, in accordance with the iconography set out by Pacheco and endorsed by his son-in-law Velázquez. Maria Elena Gómez-Moreno suggests that this was on the advice of the latter.

Martín González also looks to Velázquez for an explanation for the order to replace Bernini's *Christ*, a measure that would have been taken in order to fully enjoy its beauty in an unrestricted way i.e. without the dim light of the candelabras. Philip IV would have taken his adviser's opinion into account, particularly if, as Bonet Correra suggests, Velázquez was in charge of work on the royal mausoleum, including the sculpture.

The gilded bronze frontal was the work of the lay brothers Friar Eugenio de la Cruz and Friar Juan de la Concepción. Other outstanding elements in this royal tomb are made of identical material treated in the same way.

Between every two pilasters is a small angel bearing a candelabra. The candelabras were cast by Juan de Monaco and based on models, all of them different, by another Italian, Juan Antonio Ceroni who prepared them in 1623. A worthy addition to such a luxurious setting, the great light suspended from the semi-circular vault, is attributed to the Genoese Virgilio Fanelli.

Such was the impact of this project that in 1657, Friar Francisco de los Santos devoted almost half of his *Description of El Escorial* to the impressive burial chamber which he already refers to as a Pantheon. He made special mention of the solemn ceremony that occurred as the royal remains were conveyed to their last resting-place. In contrast to the customary absence of illustrations, de los Santos included several engravings by Pedro de Villafranca that give an overview of the great decorative project. The series of elevations and plans included one of the Genoese lamp, the epitome of that cosmopolitan splendour.

After previous decomposition in the nearby 'pudridero' (morgue), the remains of the monarchs, together with the remains of their wives if they had been mothers of kings, were placed in the urns, the former on the right of the altar and the latter on the left. With the bodies arranged in chronological order, from Charles V to Alfonso XIII, the only members of the Spanish monarchy missing from this funereal group are Philip V, his son Ferdinand VI and their respective consorts. They are buried in their corresponding foundations at La Granja de San Ildefonso and the Madrid convent of Las Salesas Reales. It should be pointed out that Isabel II, as a monarch in her own right, rests among the male figures.

GIOVANNI BATTISTA CRESCENZI. Vault covered with marbles and
jaspers and decorated with grotesques and scrolls of gilt-bronze.
VIRGILIO FANELLI. Gilt-bronze lantern.
Pantheon of Kings.

PONCIANO PONZANO

Detail of a guardian mace-bearer, carved by Jacopo Baratta.

Carrara marble and gilt-bronze.

Eighth Chamber. Pantheon of the Infantes. 1862-88.

THE PANTHEON OF THE INFANTES

The Pantheon of the Infantes came about as a result of an initiative by Isabel
II and was based on a project by José Segundo de Lema, which was approved
in 1862 but work was not completed until 1888. This pantheon occupies part
of an area of cellars that run along the perimeter of the Courtyard of the
Evangelists, specifically the part including the Sacristy and the chapter houses. According to Bustamante, they are a remarkable series of structural solutions, here hidden by the decoration of the ceiling vaults.

The ornate marble decoration of historicist inspiration was produced in Carrara by Jacopo Baralta di Leopoldo who based his work on designs by the Aragonese artist Ponciano Ponzano. In fact it gives to this originally spacious area a sensation of heavy eclecticism and makes Juan
Bautista de Toledo's design unrecognisable. For the same reason, the Pantheon of Princes, where the intrinsic richness of the material combines with
an over-elaborate design, is paradigmatic of the period. Beyond its value as
an example of mid-nineteenth century official artistic taste, the Pantheon
has great historical interest as an additional burial place for the house of
Austria and the Bourbons.

JOSÉ SEGUNDO DE LEMA, architect and PONCIANO PONZANO, sculptor. Passageway between the Eighth Chamber, with tombs of the House of Bourbon, and the Ninth Chamber, with tombs of the House of Habsburg. Pantheon of the Infantes, 1862-88.

Each of the nine colourful and richly-decorated chambers is presided over by an altar. In the first, aside from a small Neo-classical altar housing a *Descent from the Cross* by Carlo Veronese, the most outstanding features are the tombs of the dukes of Montpensier and his daughters by Aimé Millet, and those of the princesses María Josefa and Luisa Carlota of Bourbon, the latter beneath a statue by Isidro González Velázquez of Isabel II at prayer. She appears not in her role as daughter-in-law but as the founder of this pantheon. The fifth chamber contains the historicist tomb of Juan of Austria, made by Giuseppe Galleoti in accordance with Ponzano's guidelines.

Displayed on the altar of the sixth chamber is a painting entitled *The Virgin of the Veil* (1529), a much-praised work by Lavinia Fontana. This room contains the curious communal tomb of the princes from both dynasties who died before they reached adolescence, which looks like nothing so much as a twenty-sided cake in white marble. As a pantheon within a Pantheon, its form derives from Antique mausoleums. Finally, in the ninth chamber, sixteen tombs of Habsburg princes connect this 19th-century construct to the Spanish House of Austria, whose ideas lie behind the original creation of the Monastery.

The Sixth Chamber from the doorway of the Fifth Chamber.
Pantheon of the Infantes, 1862-88.

The monastic area in the Courtyard of the Evangelists

The Courtyard of the Evangelists is one of the most outstanding architectural features of the building both for the façades of the galleries and for the central shrine that gives the courtyard its name. The courtyard is of square ground-plan, has two storeys and eleven arches on each side. The lower arches are Doric and the upper ones Ionic. In fact, the courtyard is one of the few areas in the great El Escorial complex that still conforms to Juan Bautista de Toledo's designs. As Bustamente pointed out, the column reappears here, otherwise restricted to the main façade of the building, the façade of the basilica and the base of the dome.

Kubler estimated that Toledo settled on his design in 1565 but that Herrera produced a modified version later, even improving its prototype, the Theatre of Marcellus in Rome, based on a print in Serlio. Other sources indicate that Juan Bautista finalised his plans in 1566. Construction began in 1569 and did not conclude until 1579 when the parapets were put in place. With sides 58 metres long, the gigantic scale of this cloister prompted Otto Schubert to suggest that it might be the largest in the world.

The typical planted area takes the form of a cross. Although its current sobriety seem to match the architecture, it is very different from the original atmosphere at the time the monastery was founded. It is based around a small octagonal Doric building completed by a small hemispherical dome comparable to those of the basilica. Construction of the shrine began in 1586, implementing designs by Juan de Herrera. However, Father Sigüenza claimed the credit for the project. As Kubler pointed out, it was based on the Garden of Eden, with four rivers irrigating the four continents. In the opinion of Kubler, the most immediate benchmark for this *fons vitae* was probably a similar one at the convent of Santa Cruz in Coimbra, created in the 1530s. Nevertheless, in more than one sense, the building has similarities with the very large Mudejar one in the cloister of the monastery at Guadalupe, another Hieronymite foundation under royal patronage.

These heavenly references are overlaid by others explicitly concerned with the Fountain of Grace and spiritual life. Indeed the four Gospels, through the Evangelists, irrigate the parts of the world represented by the pools. Bustamante emphasizes that in spite of the extraordinary quality of the project and of the materials and the implementation, the result breaks up the impressive classical unity of the main cloister, an essential part of the monastery from the outset. He goes on to say that this can be explained in terms of the process of disguise, consecration, symbolization or mythologization of the building, specifically through Father Sigüenza's proposal, "which had the great value of its richness and complexity, as it combined biblical, and mythological tradition with religion and politics".

Using Herrera's designs as a starting point, a wooden model was prepared in 1586. As Bustamante stated, there must have been debate on the decoration. The king was as keenly interested in plans for the shrine as in the decorative cycles of paintings and his was the last word. In 1589, with the fountain and the water tank completed, Juan Bautista Monegro was commissioned with the task of creating the figures of the evangelists. These were not presented until 1593. Apart from their iconographic function, these figures are both dignified and restrained, appropriately subordinate to the grandeur of the Herreresque pavilion.

Around the Courtyard of the Evangelists, the galleries of the main cloister are decorated by a series of fifty-four frescoes on the theme of the Story of the Redemption, from the *Birth of the Virgin* to the *Last Judgement,* arranged in order starting from the door leading into the basilica known as the Procession Door. Pellegrino Tibaldi was commissioned to paint these compositions between 1586 and 1590. According to Sylvie

The Fountain of Saint John the Evangelists which feeds the north-east pond.

Tempietto of the Courtyard of the Evangelists.

JUAN BAUTISTA MONEGRO

Saint John the Evangelist. Detail with the Gospel written in Latin and Syriac: «Truly I say to you that
if you are not reborn with water and the Holy Spirit you cannot enter into the Kingdom of God.»
Marble, 1589-93.
Tempietto of the Courtyard of the Evangelists.

Béguin, the scenes take place in a slow and solemn succession of rhythmical pauses, reflecting the processional atmosphere of the place.

Situated in the centre of the western gallery, the main stairway is one of the most distinctive architectural features of the monastery and also one of the most controversial. It has a square ground-plan, 12 metres long and 23 metres high. Regarded as being "of great power and beauty" by contemporaries, it was a new type of stairway on account of its open, box-like structure which projected beyond the roof, and for the grouping together of its steps into flights or sections with a main, central flight and two lateral ones in the opposite direction. This arrangement was later termed 'imperial'.

The overall result did not correspond with Juan Bautista de Toledo's plans, as he had wanted a conventual staircase parallel to the wall in the Spanish style. Neither did it constitute the specific, personal and global alternative that his rivals or successors aspired to. On the basis of the requirements of location and perimeter specified by the author of the universal design there ensued a confused redesign process whose vicissitudes have given rise to prolonged controversy.

In 1567, Juan de Herrera carried out a royal consultation concerning a design for the stairway presented by Giovan Battista Castello, 'El

Bergamasco'. In addition we know from records that Herrera was involved in the project from 1571 onwards. Thus, the debate involves those who credit Herrera with the proposals and those who come down fairly confidently on the side of Castello. Javier Ribera favours the latter whereas other scholars opt for Herrera, including Wilkinson-Zerner, Íñiguez Almech and Fernando Marías.

On the basis of a rigorous analysis, Bustamante adopted an intermediate position, taking all the candidates into account. The staircase itself could be the work of Castelló but the upper and lower sections of the structure are attributed to Herrera and Toledo respectively. In 1571, Herrera opened up the stairwell, the brilliant culmination of a piece of empirical teamwork which comes across to the unsuspecting viewer as a coherent and highly individual project.

Under the arches on the second level, Luca Cambiaso depicted a series of *The Apparitions of Christ* whose stylistic consistency does not rule out a second, subsidiary contributor in the form of Pellegrino Tibaldi. Once again, the chilly uniformity of these 16th-century frescoes is broken up by the extremely Baroque work of Luca Giordano who decorated the friezes and a vault in 1692-93. The friezes have three scenes from *The Battle of Saint Quentin* and another more interesting scene of *The Construction of the Monastery,* with its founder taking an explicit role. Above this institutional tribute a vast *Glory* stretches out across the vault. It alludes to the painting of the same name by Titian which also includes the figures of Charles V and Philip II. Outside this heavenly orbit on the middle lunette of the western wall and opposite the observer ascending the staircase, Charles II presents his wife, Mariana of Neuburg and his mother Mariana of Austria. The inscription accompanying this apotheosis fittingly reads *La Gloria de la Monarquía española* (The Glory of the Spanish Monarchy).

In the southern sector of the same western part of the cloister, is the Old or Borrowed Church, a temporary building used as the monastery church from 1571 until the completion of the basilica in 1586. Its three nobly designed marble altars have been preserved unaltered. The largest of these

LUCA GIORDANO

The Glorification of the Spanish Monarchy, 1692-93.

Vault of the Main Staircase.

The Prioral Room. Chapter Houses.

Niccolò Granello, Fabrizio Castello,

Lazzaro Tavarone and Orazio Cambiaso: vault frescoes.

houses *The Martyrdom of Saint Lawrence* by Titian, a vast canvas measuring 4.4 by 3.2 metres. According to Freedberg, Augusto Gentili and Charles Hope, it is one of Titian's most important late works, while Hope also considers it his most important night piece. It is signed on the grill and was painted between 1564 and 1567 following a composition developed shortly prior to that for the Jesuits in Venice but here with more pronounced and moving chiaroscuro and an almost expressionist palette.

The southern side of the cloister houses the Vicarial and Prioral Chapter Houses. The Prior's Cell, behind the second of these, and the central or joint hallway running through the two chapter houses complete the courtyard's magnificent southern. Here, the unified decorative scheme of the vaults is enhanced by the splendid canvases and panel paintings that still hang on the walls. Taking advantage of the optimum conditions offered by these fine rooms and the neighbouring Sacristy, Velázquez re-organized the monastery's art collections into a picture gallery (of which the most important works are now in the Prado). Nevertheless, much of what remains both in the chapter houses and in other annexes continues to reflect the high quality that characterized this historical collection.

Vault frescoes, detail of the decoration with grotesque motifs.
Prioral Room.
Chapter Houses.

The hallway or foyer is a square space with three arched openings leading onto each of the large rooms. In 1581, the vault was painted with a decorative fresco by Nicolo Granello and Francesco da Urbino, with a design repeating that of the Prioral Cell. Both chapter houses are 22 metres long, 9 metres wide and 8 metres high, reflecting the size of the religious community. As the bench running around the rooms indicates, they were intended as assembly halls for the one hundred monks. These spaces were lit by thermal windows while their ceilings were painted with grotesque ornament comparable to that in The Hall of Battles. When that hall was completed in 1585 the same Genoese team were given the task of decorating the chapter houses. The team consisted of Nicolo Granello, Fabrizio Castello, Lazzaro Taverone and Orazio Cambiaso who finished the work the following year.

Decorative work on the Prior's Lower Cell was carried out in 1581-82 by Francesco da Urbino, perhaps in the collaboration with the aforementioned Castello and Granello, with subsequent amendments by the latter with Cincinnato. In the opinion of Von der Osten Sacken, Cincinnato's central roundel, *The Judgement of Solomon*, compares Solomon with Philip II as founder of a temple.

JOSÉ DE RIBERA,
"EL ESPAÑOLETO"
(Left)
The Penitent Saint Jerome.
(Right)
*Saint Francis receiving the
Stigmata, 1642.*
Vicarial Room.
Chapter Houses.

    Saint Jerome in Penitence by Titian presides over the Vicarial Chapter House. The date of the painting, approximately 1570, is a matter of debate and Wethey puts it forward to 1575. This badly damaged canvas has a splendid landscape with the rich expressionism characteristic of Titian's last phase. Alongside are two flower paintings by Mario Nuzzi, called "dei Fiori", and two hermit saints by Ribera: *Saint Jerome the Penitent* is a damaged work and of questionable authorship, while *Saint Paul,* also known as *Saint Onophrio,* was signed and dated by Ribera in 1639 but its poor condition prevents us from making out the inscription.

    Two magnificent canvases, also by Ribera, have been hung on the large wall opposite the windows. *Saint Francis receiving the Stigmata* has been attributed to Ribera by Mayer, albeit with reservations. The true identity of the painter had been questioned due to later overpainting. However, as Pérez Sánchez pointed out, following the recent restoration of this superb picture, the identity of the artist has become evident. It is signed and dated 1642. *Jacob with Laban's Flock,* signed and dated 1682, indicates Ribera's move away from realism under the influence of Velázquez.

    Velázquez is represented in the Vicarial Chapter House, alongside these works by Ribera, in the form of an important work from his first Italian trip: *Joseph's blood-stained Coat brought to Jacob.* This was painted in Rome in 1630 and reached the Escorial around 1657 via the Buen Retiro Palace. The canvas has been cut down on both sides which distorts the perspective. Although it is of similar format to the contemporary canvas by the artist of *Vulcan's Forge,* they are not necessarily a pair.

Diego de Silva Velázquez

Joseph's blood-stained Coat brought to Jacob, 1630 (detail).

Vicarial Room. Chapter Houses.

EL GRECO (DOMENIKOS THEOTOKOPOULOS)
The Dream of Philip II, c. 1577-79.
Vicarial Room. Chapter Houses.

According to López-Rey, Velázquez clarifies the space surrounding the figures by emphasizing the geometrical pattern of the paving, a perspectival device which, according to Gerstenberg, he may have derived from Daniello Barbari's treatise, although it might have been Tintoretto who first used it to achieve dramatic effects. Velázquez himself may have subsequently repainted the canvas in some areas. The canvas was restored in 1989.

Three of the most distinguished paintings by El Greco hang between the windows. The first picture is *The Adoration of the Name of Jesus* or *The Allegory of The Holy League* which is signed and was painted around 1577-79. Despite its small size, its monumental approach to space has led some historians to interpret it as an initial design for one of the wall paintings in the building. It was the first work offered by El Greco to the King, whether or not as a commission is unknown. After a meticulous study of the painting in 1939-40, Anthony Blunt reached the now accepted conclusion that besides evoking the Adoration of the Name of Jesus, it is an allegory of the alliance formed in 1571 by Spain, the Pope and Venice in opposition to the Turks.

The kneeling figures of Philip II, Pius V and Doge Mocenigo give thanks for the victory at Lepanto, also commemorated in other works in El Escorial which depict the victory in a narrative mode. The figure with the sword is probably an idealized portrait of Juan of Austria, the hero of the naval combat. In 1657 Father Francisco de los Santos described the picture as El Greco's *Glory*. In spite of its technique and ambitious composition and iconography, the painting did not displease Philip II. However, the King fell out with the artist over the next royal commission.

Saint Peter and *Saint Ildefonso* form a matching pair of paintings, painted by El Greco around 1610-14, apparently as a part of the decoration of the Ovalle Chapel in the church of San Vicente in Toledo. Their presence in El Escorial had already been recorded by the end of the seventeenth century. The fluent, free-flowing brushwork reaches heights of great virtuosity in the apparel worn by Saint Ildefonso.

School of
HIERONYMOUS BOSCH
The Temptations of Saint Anthony, 16ᵗʰ-century.
Lower Prioral Cell.
Chapter Houses.

In contrast to the varied contents of the Vicarial chapter house, the Prior's is basically decorated with canvases from the Venetian school. *The Agony in the Garden* by Titian presides over the altar. Painted in about 1556, the deterioration in the condition of the picture prevents us from accurately determining the extent of the contribution made by the artist's studio. The Prado has another version of the painting, which was originally at El Escorial and has a broader narrative scope including the scene portraying the capture of Christ, with the prayer scene relegated to the background. *The Rest on the Flight into Egypt* was painted in about 1535 by Titian's workshop, albeit with his intervention.

The Last Supper was painted between 1557 and 1565 and was intended for the monastery's refectory. The canvas reveals considerable collaboration (albeit much disputed by experts), in common with much of Titian's work at the period. Following its recent restoration, the picture has acquired qualities that were previously indiscernible as a result of its poor condition. Moreover, the canvas was drastically cut so that it would fit into its place, affecting the balance of the composition which is now rather narrow in relation to its wide architectural setting.

An excellent late work by Titian is the *Saint John the Baptist* of around 1560. The saint's mystical expression contrasts with that in the

TITIAN

The Last Supper, c. 1557-65.

Lower Prioral Cell.

Chapter Houses.

more sensual and wordly version of around 1540. Tintoretto is represented by two excellent paintings from the same period. *Esther before Ahasuerus,* of 1547, was a controversial picture until the evident identity of the painter took precedence over its poor condition. Another version of the canvas is at Hampton Court (London). *Christ and Mary Magadalen in the Pharisee's House,* dating from between 1546 and 1547, has enjoyed a similar critical history. An additional drawback is that it shows signs of the typical re-painting carried out in order to brighten up canvases darkened by time. According to Ruiz Gómez, it must have been subjected to this form of 'restoration' soon after reaching the monastery while Velázquez was at work on the decorative programme.

The work of Veronese is represented by *Christ's Descent into Limbo* which might be alternatively titled *Christ, accompanied by the Parents from Limbo, visits his Mother.* Although critics generally reject this picture, Ruiz Gómez stresses the notable quality and the Veronesian style of the two main figures.

Also in the Prior's Hall are *The Eritrean Sibyl* and *The Prophet Elijah* by Moretto da Brescia. In addition, the lecterns used for reading the Epistles and the Gospels are on display in the middle of the chapter house: these were made in 1571 by Juan Simón of Antwerp.

Charles V's portable altarpiece presides over the Prior's Cell. This is an exquisite piece of work in silver-gilt, enamelling and wood carving. The apparent unity masks the possible influence of various stylistic tendencies.

ANONYMOUS GERMAN

Portable altar of the Emperor Charles V. Chased silver and silver-gilt,
enamelling, wood with ebony veneer. First half of the 16th century.
Lower Prioral Cell. Chapter Houses.

The Italianate style evident in the reliefs and the Apostles gives way in the three upper elements to a later, more international Mannerist style. It has been suggested that the arrangement of the main altarpiece in the basilica may have been influenced by this work.

Also on display here are panel paintings by Hieronymus Bosch. The triptych entitled *The Haywain* is signed on the lower edge of the left frame. Another version of the painting is in the Prado but was originally at El Escorial. The unsatisfactory condition of both versions frustrates any attempt to determine which one was produced first. Although the association of worldly vanity with hay echoes one of the Psalms of David taken up by Isaiah, it is also recorded in Flemish tradition.

Flanking the central haywain, to the left is *The Earthly Paradise* and, to the right, *Hell*. The reverse sides of these lateral wings represent

HIERONYMUS BOSCH
The Haywain, triptych.
Lower Prioral Cell.
Chapter Houses.

The Sacristy from the north wall.

NICCOLÒ GRANELLO : vault frescoes.

The Path of Life. Bermejo Martínez has summed up the message of the triptych in the following way: the fall of angels and of men sends evil into the world, exalting transient pleasures and thus provoking punishment in hell.

The Crowning with Thorns is generally considered to be an autograph work. It must have been the central panel in another triptych, as shown by the Valencia copy. The circular scene contains half-length figures and depicts Christ in the company of a number of characters, three with grotesque expressions and gestures. Both the meaning and the date of the painting have given rise to greatly differing opinions. It may be a political satire or it may symbolise political and religious power. Many possible dates have been put forward, ranging from the beginning to the end of Bosch's career. Bermejo Martínez has estimated that the picture dates from the middle of his career. Lastly, the panel entitled *The Route to Calvary* has an extremely beautiful background landscape.

The Sacristy (not open to visitors) and the Ante-Sacristy form a part of the eastern wing of the Main Cloister. The sacristy ceiling was painted in fresco by Niccolo Granello in 1583-84. The eastern wall has a finely-made washstand or fountain of marble and jasper in the shape of a small façade with five recesses. Granello also painted the vault of the Sacristy whose decoration, reaching up to 11 metres high, features a series of octagons between transverse friezes without a central motif, painted against a huge background 30 metres long by 9 metres wide.

COURT WORKSHOP
Chalice. Cast and chased silver with silver-gilt, end of the 16th century. Sacristy.

The Sacristy walls are decorated by some of the best paintings in the monastery. Their historical importance is best illustrated by the magnificent canvas of the altarpiece. First, however, we should look at several works by Luca Giordano, but above all, the *Christ on the Cross* by Titian. This is always regarded as an authentic work from late in his career, around 1565. Incomprehensibly, it is viewed as a poor painting by certain critics, but as Ruiz Gómez suggested, this impression may have arisen from the dim lighting in the room. However, in the opinion of Wethey, it is one of Titian's masterpieces. On the other hand, there is no authoritative support for the claim that Ribera painted *The Liberation of Saint Peter,* a modest copy of the original in Dresden. Nevertheless we should point out that the copy differs from the original composition in some respects.

The *Altarpiece of the Sacred Form* is the result of very different historical events. Rudolph II of Germany donated to Philip II a host that had been desecrated by heretics and had miraculously remained pure. More than a century later, Charles I had to carry out papal penitence in order to secure the reversal of a sentence of excommunication

Embroidery workshop of the San Lorenzo
de El Escorial Monastery.
(Left) Chasuble of the Vestments of the
Life of Christ.
Silk embroidered in burnished gold
thread. Second period, c. 1577.
(Right)
FRIAR LORENZO DE MONTSERRAT
Pluvial cape and attached cape of
the Vestments of *Saint Lawrence*.
Silk and silver thread, sequins,
velvet and embroidery.
First period, c. 1569.
Sacristy.

passed against those who had invaded the monastery in 1677 in pursuit of the royal favourite Valenzuela. Charles therefore built a chapel in which to keep this revered eucharistic revelation.

Designed by José del Olmo it was completed in 1691 according to records. It is a typical example of an altarpiece with a device for lowering the great canvas-backdrop by means of a system of pulleys in order to reveal the monstrance in the small chapel behind, no less richly decorated than the front. A large, heavy Baroque "machine" of composite order, it consists of alternating cut marble and jasper with decorative work in gilt-bronze, the latter by the Italian Francesco Filipini. The white marble, lateral low reliefs are attributed to Domenico Guidi. Two of them show scenes of blasphemy and subsequent repentance and conversion of the heretics while two more above depict the presentation of the prodigious wafer and the king of Spain accepting it.

The Adoration of the Sacred Form was signed and dated by Claudio Coello in 1690 with a Latin inscription, although execution of the painting had taken at least five years. This is the masterpiece of the artist who became the leader of the Madrid school following the death of Velázquez. The painting represents the solemn and appropriate splendid ceremony that took place on October 19, 1680 as the host was taken to a new chapel.

This extraordinary group portrait effectively constituted a snapshot of the Spanish court. The painting has aroused much debate as to the way in which the artist intended to use space in the composition. As Martín Soria says, it is "a vast aerial extension of the Sacristy". But, in Sullivan's view, Coello did not intend to extend the perspective of the room beyond its physical limits, since this is not done by means of illusion but, instead, by reflecting what is seen from the canvas itself. Neither was he aiming for a mirror effect, as the positions of the pictures and the windows are not reversed.

The altar acts as a screen or veil for the small chapel of the Sacred Form, which is only revealed on very special occasions. When the great ceremonial stage is lowered and completely disappears, the magnificent *Crucifix* by Pietro Tacca is visible on the reliquary. Made of fire-gilt bronze, it stands 190 centimetres high. It was initially intended for the Pantheon. According to Martín González, it must have been commissioned prior to 1635, the year that saw the death of Crescenzi who was responsible for the decoration of the royal mausoleum.

The current Neo-gothic tabernacle, also of gilt-bronze, was made between 1829 and 1834 after a design by the painter Vicente López, replacing one that disappeared during the Napoleonic wars.

The Royal Library

Artist known as the
«ANÓNIMO DE LA CÁMARA REGIA»
Two ladies playing chess, dressed in the
Gothic style (with blouses embroidered
with precious stones, edged pelisses, cloaks
and high headdresses supported by a
parchment framework).
Book of the Games of Chess, Dice and Trick-track of King Alfonso X the Wise, 1283.
Royal Library.

Royal Library. Main Room or Room of the
Printed Books, 1586-1591.
PELLEGRINO TIBALDI: frescoes.
JUAN DE HERRERA: design of the bookshelves.
ANTONIO SANTUCCI: armillary sphere, c. 1582.

As its location, decoration, contents and, consequently its historical role indicate, the Royal Library is not an annex of the monastery although it provides a direct service to the monastery and the school. Rather, it is a royal institution incorporated into the complex functions of a building that also serves as a residence for the sovereign. When the library was founded, voices were raised in opposition to the supposedly profane decoration, judged to be unsuitable for a monastery, especially a Hieronymite one. In response, Father Sigüenza asserted that the library belonged to the King and was open to all. In view of the fact that although the library was royal, it was also used by the monks, the cautious friar added that the writings of Antiquity were full of subjects conducive to pious meditation.

Prior to the El Escorial project, the concept of a great library as the fount of all knowledge and a source of prestige for the authorities had emerged in mid-sixteenth-century Spain from a different ideological starting-point. The report submitted by Juan Pérez de Castro to the King in 1556 proposed the setting up of a great public library in Valladolid, the location of

IBN AL-DURAYHIM
AL-MAWSILI
(Above) *Fish,* folio 118.
(Below) «On the species of
fish and aquatic animals
that swim with them»
(calligraphy in gold),
Description of the types of
fish (cartouche), folio 117v.
Book of the Uses of Animals.
Illuminated manuscript,
parchment.
Arabic-Mamluk, 1354.
Royal Library.

the Court at that time. Considering that the promotion of the capital city and the monastery were parallel aims, it is surprising that Philip II regarded the library as less than ideal from the ideological and cultural standpoint of the emerging nation state.

The distancing of a collection which, on account of its ambiguous nature in the context of El Escorial, never became an institution in its own right, gave rise to the myth of the '*bibliotafio*' and the corresponding controversy. This debate lasted as long as the Hieronymite community and still continues to arouse historical debate. Arguments continue as to the advisability of the decision made by Philip II and, in particular, about the results, which many believe were far better than would be expected from the negative image of an under-used or even dead library.

As with so many other aspects of the foundation, the eventual structure of the library derived from a long, accumulative process originally harbouring a very different purpose. Initially, the monarch did not intend to create a mixed library for both the monastery and the court. The first plans envisaged the library only as an integral part of the monastery. But, in 1564, when the number of monks doubled and the number of chapter houses increased accordingly, the library had to be moved from the main cloister where it was just another section of the building.

Aside from this trajectory, the library began to develop on a separate basis. This began in 1579 when Philip II, encouraged by the spirit of the Council of Trent, resolved to promote and strengthen the library, the seminary and the school. It became a Royal Library but with a heavy emphasis on its monastic and didactic aspects, this combined mission coexisting with the its role as a utilitarian instrument of orthodoxy in the hands of the monks. Its very location, in the corner of the entry porch of the main façade constitutes a link between the school and the monastery and illustrates this double functional connection which, in theory, is no obstacle to its secular objectives.

On an axis with the basilica and the King's House, the Library thus expressing the indissoluble union of knowledge, faith and power that forms the basis for the Catholic Monarchy. In accordance with

ANONYMOUS

The Adoration of the Magi, with the Emperor Charles V depicted as King Melchior.

Breviarium Caroli V Imperatoris, vol. I, folio 183 v.

Illuminated manuscript, parchment, second quarter of the 16ᵗʰ century. Royal Library.

the privileged location of the library building behind the great façade, straddling the vestibule and presiding over the entrance to the monument, its interior decoration is as rich and complete as its collection of books.

In order to establish the original collection, Philip II not only contributed his own private collection consisting of more than 4,000 volumes, but also others which had belonged to various royal patrons as well as public institutions. For example, 133 volumes came from the Royal Chapel of Granada, 139 banned titles came from the Inquisition and other books were contributed by the Monastery of Poblet.

Purchases and donations added extraordinary collections belonging to scholars, professionals and courtiers such as that of the ambassador Diego Hurtado de Mendoza with its splendid Italian editions, rare incunabula and manuscripts, or the collections of the chronicler Jerónimo de Zurita, the Marquis of Vélez, the humanist and archbishop of Tarragona, Antonio Agustín, Juan de Herrera himself and Benito Arias Montano, with Arab, Hebrew and Oriental works. Over 10,000 books were assembled at this initial phase. Interestingly, one of the collections incorporated into the library at this time was that of doctor Juan Páez de Castro, the proponent of the Valladolid public library.

Although the first royal consignments date back to 1565 when the project had still not been redefined, the library was not officially set up until 1576. In that year, the library was entrusted to the monastic community and Arias Montano took on the task of classifying the books with the assistance of Friar Juan de San Jerónimo and Father Sigüenza, who would subsequently take on the role of director. Philip II searched for books within Spain and through various agents. His enquiries in the Low Countries were conducted by the tireless Arias Montano. Similarly, the chronicler Ambrosio de Morales selected manuscripts for El Escorial in the cathedrals and monasteries of León, Galicia and Asturias.

In accordance with the humanistic nature of the building, an upper hall houses a gallery first mentioned in 1587 of 171 portraits of illustrious men. Scholars, emperors, kings and other notable figures, both pagan and Christian, come together here. To this end, attempts were made to secure copies of the most highly-considered originals and Arias Montano used an intermediary in Rome to oversee the production of a vast series of reproductions of paintings scattered throughout the whole of Italy. As Von der Osten Sacken pointed out, this collection of paintings reveals the same desire for a systematic unity evident in other decorations or collections at the monastery. This even extended to what we might term the commemorative attitude of the King, prompting him to order thirty thousand masses for the deceased.

Philip III granted the library the privilege that was later known as *depósito legal* (legal deposit), a measure that was never well-received by the printers. In 1612, the library belonging to Muley Zidón, Sultan of Morocco, was unexpectedly captured in a naval engagement. This resulted in the arrival of approximately 4,000 codices which, for the most part, would unfortunately be lost in the fire of 1671 despite being moved to the main upper cloister for safety. The so-called manuscript library, next to the main library, also suffered damage in the fire, but the principal library was spared.

GERARD DE HORENBOULD
OF GHENT
Illuminated text with a floral
mosaic border.
Breviary of the Empress
Elizabeth of Portugal,
Folio 167v.
Illuminated manuscript,
parchment.
Flemish School, 16th-century.
Royal Library.

IBN AL-DURAYHIM AL-MAWSILI

«THE BLESSED BOOK IS FINISHED. . The humble servant of the Highest compiled it…, helped by the grace of God
He completed its marvellous and rare designs and engravings. THROUGH THE GRACE AND WITH THE HELP OF GOD».
Book of the Uses of Animals, Colophon I, folio 153v. Illuminated manuscript, parchment. Arabic-Mamluk, 1354.
Royal Library.

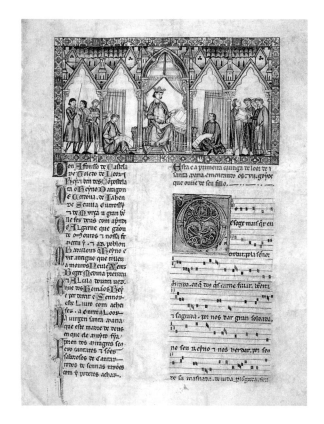

Work on the publication of catalogues began in the eighteenth century during the reign of Charles III. Following the French invasion, Joseph Bonaparte combined this Royal Library with the Royal Library of Madrid, making the new institution a truly national one controlled by the government rather than the Crown. In 1814, Ferdinand VII gave the library back to the monastery, not without protests from those who considered it more beneficial to leave it with the Court. On February 14 1836, a decree declared that the library was owned by the State and that it was subject to inspection by the Royal Academy of History. As José Quevedo said thirteen years later in his *Description* of the building, we should be grateful to this "literary and essentially conservative body" not only for maintaining the library intact but also for improvements and even additions. The 1847 decree instructed the association of chaplains to occupy and look after the monastery, substituting the suppressed community of monks. Subsequently, the Library was once more placed under the auspices of the Crown.

The library is easily the most splendid room in El Escorial. Besides the manuscript library, there was another for banned or reserved

ANONYMOUS

(Left) *The Visitation.* Book of Hours. Illuminated manuscript, parchment. Flemish, post-Burgundian School, after 1475.
(Right) Cantiga I, «The King declares himself troubadour of the Virgin and sings the Seven Couplets in Praise of the Mother of God».
Cantigas of Saint Mary, folio 5. Illuminated manuscript, parchment. Hispano-French School, after 1279.
Royal Library.

books, common practice until well into the nineteenth century. The principal room has five doors opening onto La Lonja and seven onto the Kings' Courtyard. The magnificent main hall, which splendidly fulfils the role of a late Renaissance court library, is 54 metres long, 9 metres wide and 10 metres high at the highest point of its barrel vault with lunettes. The richness of the shelving and the fresco paintings make it one of the most brilliantly resolved and executed buildings of its time. Like the Vatican library, it has proved to be a classic creation of its type, influencing numerous projects.

In contrast to the cool paving in white and grey marble, the vault and the frieze display wonderful decorative work by Pellegrino Tibaldi, unequalled outside Italy. As Sylvie Béguin stated, in 1586. Tibaldi introduced a modified Michelangelesque aesthetic into Spain which discarded the secular and worldly tendencies evident in one strand of the great artist's output, consistent with the ideals of Philip II. This encounter between the neo-Michelangelesque style and the Christian humanism of the Catholic Monarchy is nowhere better reflected than in the El Escorial library. Here, on account of the subject, Tibaldi follows his model more closely than in other works.

This difficult and laborious project began with the preparatory work in 1586 and was completed in 1591. The chronicler of the foundation of the monastery, Friar José de Sigüenza, was responsible for the wide-ranging and complex iconographic programme, filled with references in an ambitious symbolic synthesis of knowledge, from Philosophy to Theology and including the seven liberal arts. As Von der Osten Sacken pointed out, although Sigüenza claimed all the credit for the plan, it can be assumed that it was the result of close collaboration between the painter, the architect, the librarian, and the King himself, as reflected in a sketch of the frescoes with annotations by Juan de Herrera.

Von der Osten Sacken was also convinced that Benito Arias Montano, Sigüenza's predecessor as librarian, also intervened. The almost exclusively pagan and Jewish sources of the scenes on the friezes may be attributable to him.

Royal Library. Main Room or Room of the Printed Books. Frescoes on the north end wall, 1586-91.

Lunette: PELLEGRINO TIBALDI. . *Philosophy, mother of all the sciences, between Aristotle, Plato, Seneca and Socrates, the Ancient philosophers.* Frieze: BARTOLOMEO CARDUCCI, TIBERIO RONCHI. *The School of Athens: Stoics and Sceptics.*

JOHANNES BLAEU: celestial globe, c. 1660.

Royal Library. Main Room or Room of the Printed Books. Frescoes on the south end wall, 1586-91.

Lunette: PELLEGRINO TIBALDI. *Theology, supreme science of Revelation, between the Four Doctors of the Latin Church, Saints Jerome, Ambrose, Gregory the Great and Augustine.* Frieze: BARTOLOMEO CARDUCCI, TIBERIO RONCHI. *The Council of Nicea.*

ANTONIO SANTUCCI: armillary sphere, c. 1582.

As the library pertained to both the monastery and the palace, there was a strong connection between theological and secular studies. The latter was regarded not only as an encyclopaedic quest for knowledge or scientific research. Rather, it was also seen from the political standpoint of the need for information. Nevertheless, Taylor considered that it involved an inevitably hermetic aspect due to the Salomonic connection.

The two large lunettes on the end walls have representations of *Philosophy* and *Theology*. The northern one, on the College side where the pictorial cycle begins, shows Philosophy as a female personification pointing to a globe of the world among the figures of Aristotle, Plato, Socrates and Seneca. Below the female figure, the appropriate section of the frieze depicts *The School of Athens*, divided between the Stoics and the Sceptics. The uniform height of the frieze is 2.25 metres throughout the whole hall.

The opposite southern side adjoins the monastery area. Appropriately, therefore, Theology appears with a crown and a halo pointing to the Holy Scriptures among the Fathers of the Latin Church. In a very direct reference to the cause of the Counter-Reformation, the frieze here depicts *The Council of Nicaea*. Presided over by the Emperor Constantine, the Council condemned the heresy of Arrius and set out the articles of faith.

This twofold system of a main scene and an additional one matches the characteristics of the vault. The seven sections of the vault have a corresponding illustrated story on the frieze. These comprise female allegories of the seven liberal arts in accordance with the medieval categoriza-

PELLEGRINO TIBALDI
(Left)
Dialectic, part of the *Three Liberal Arts of Eloquence* –Trivium.
(Right)
Music, with the swan of Apollo, god of music, surrounded by *ignudi* (nudes) with musical scores and instruments, from *the Four Liberal Arts of Mathematics* – Quadrivium.
Frescoes on the vault, 1586-91.
Royal Library. Main Room or Room of the Printed Books.

PELLEGRINO TIBALDI
Detail of *Astrology,*
surrounded by *ignudi* (nudes)
with calculations and
instruments for astronomy
from *the Four Liberal Arts of
Mathematics* – Quadrivium.
Frescoes on the vault,
1586-91.
Royal Library. Main Room
or Room of the Printed
Books.

tion of the Trivium (Grammar, Rhetoric and Logic) and the Quadrivium (Arithmetic, Music, Geometry and Astrology). The design makes use of the lunettes to add the figures of two illustrious exponents of each of these intellectual activities, positioned on either side of the personifications on the ceiling.

Fourteen episodes thus make up the large decorative band which runs under the cornice. It ranges from the worlds of Egypt and Babylon to that of the Bible, and onto classical antiquity (including mythology) and finally to Christianity, only represented by Dionysius the Aeropagite and the still unconverted Saint Augustine. Some critics have been surprised at the unusual subject matter. Thus, in the fourth section which deals with Arithmetic, we are shown the gymnosophists absorbed in their futile calculations about the soul.

The decoration of the hall has been interpreted in secretive terms, with sustained speculation that astrology is the most likely explanation. However, Father Sigüenza made it clear that he included astrology precisely in order to show the divine wish that men should no longer be afraid of the influence of the stars.

Geometrical and grotesque decoration mark out the structure of this remarkable pictorial apotheosis, which is always regarded as a tribute to the vault in the Sistine Chapel. Moreover, the stories represented on the frieze could be an echo of the work carried out in Rome by the Ghirlandaio studio. Ceán, patriotically intent on favouring Tibaldo, emphasised the originality of his colouring as a feature in which he surpassed Michelangelo. Perhaps this comparison should be reconsidered in the light of recent and controversial restoration work on the Sistine Chapel which has revealed Michelangelo as a great colourist. Tibaldi's work was firmly rooted in that of Michelangelo but here, as García-Frias has suggested, Tibaldi demonstrates his own style in combining various elements from Emilian and Roman artistic ambits.

The identity of the artist who created the scenes on the frieze is still difficult to ascertain. Although they have traditionally been attributed to Bartolomeo Carducci, known in Spain as Bartolomé Carducho, there are no documents to corroborate this. In the opinion of García-Frías, the vault and the lunettes were designed solely by Tibaldi, but in the frescoes under the cornice he worked with artists such as Carducho and Tiberio Ronchi.

The shelves with their Doric order are magnificent pieces of architecture, made by José Flecha, Juan Senén and Martín de Gamboa from designs by Juan de Herrera. Springing from a red jasper base, the bookcas-

JUAN DE HERRERA: section of bookshelving with Doric order between two doors,
made by Giuseppe Flecha, Juan Senén and Martín Gamboa, 1586-91.
Tropical hardwoods, acana and orange wood. Gilt-metal grill (18th-century).
Royal Library. Main Room or Room of the Printed Books.

es use rich materials appropriate to their contents, with the shelves of tropical hardwoods in their natural colours, the shafts of the columns are in acana wood and the capitals in orange wood.

The books face outwards so that the paper can 'breathe'. Visible through the 18th-century wire grilles, the golden edges of the pages merge into the splendid setting to create an image of warm solemnity. "Thus, the room appears beautiful as from the top to the bottom it is either painted or gilded". This unifying effect of gilding is also used in the main chapel, the Pantheon, and the Royal Library, the three interior spaces with the greatest decorative and symbolic content in the monastery.

The five greyish-brown marble tables date from the time of the monastery's foundation and are positioned around the room, while the two porphyry octagonal tables were produced by Bartolomé Zumbigo in about 1660. A wide-ranging collection of globes, celestial spheres, maps, astrolabes and other instruments was displayed on them, corresponding to the library's role as a centre for scientific research. This scientific past can be seen in other exhibits such as the armillary sphere constructed according to the Ptolemaic system by Antonio Santucci in about 1582, and the terrestrial and celestial globes by Jean Blaeu dating from around 1660. Also on display is a lodestone apparently found during excavation work before the foundations of the building were laid.

Important pieces of cabinet-making are the late 18th-century coins and medals cabinet inlaid in ebony and boxwood, and small Baroque doorway leading to the monastery area, the latter made in 1622.

The room contains several royal portraits that are interesting from both an artistic and an iconographic point of view. Since El Escorial was founded, it has housed a portrait of *Philip II* as an elderly man, possibly by Pantoja de la Cruz. Painted at some time between 1593 and 1598, the year of the King's death, this is the most expressive late image of him. A portrait of *Philip III* in armour bears the signature of Pantoja with the date 1609 although it is believed to

ALBRECHT DÜRER
The Nativity.
From the Life of the Virgin Series, folio 145.
Woodcut on paper.
German School, 1511.
Royal Library.

JUAN PANTOJA DE LA CRUZ (attributed to)

Philip II, c. 1593-98.

Royal Library. Main Room or Room of the Printed Books.

JUAN PANTOJA DE LA CRUZ (attributed to)

(Left) *Charles V,* 1608.

(Right) *Philip III,* c. 1609.

Royal Library. Main Room or Room of the Printed Books.

DIEGO DE SILVA VELÁZQUEZ
Philip IV, c. 1632-33.
National Gallery, London.
In the Royal Library until
the Peninsular wars.

JUAN CARREÑO DE MIRANDA
Charles II, c. 1675.
Royal Library. Main Room or Room of the Printed Books.

BARTOLOMEO CARDUCCI
(attributed to)
Father José de Sigüenza.
Royal Library.
Main Room or Room of the
Printed Books.

have been painted somewhat earlier. This portrait was hung on the orders of the monarch himself who also commissioned the portrait of his grandfather, the *Emperor Charles V* in armour, in another work by Pantoja (1608), now known to be a copy of a lost work by Titian. To comply with the demands of what was developing into a series of dynastic portraits, the next space was reserved for a picture of *Philip IV in Brown and Silver* by Velázquez, now in the National Gallery, London. After its disappearance in the Napoleonic wars, it was replaced by a fine portrait of Charles II, a characteristic work by Carreño de Miranda dated around 1675.

Finally, the portrait of Father Sigüenza was painted in 1602, probably by Bartolomé Carducho, leaving us with a record of the man who worked as the chronicler of the foundation and who succeeded Arias Montano as its librarian.

Either as a historical library or as a library-museum, the El Escorial collection comprises 40,000 printed volumes, and a large number of manuscripts of which 2,000 are Arab, 580 Greek, 72 are Hebrew and more than 2,000 in Latin and other languages. Famous for its manuscripts, the library is also noted for its incunabula (books printed before 1500) and for its bindings. Particularly outstanding are the books bound during the Renaissance, as Philip II's decorative programmes extended even into this field.

Among the treasures in the library is an example of Mozarabic illumination: the *Commentary on The Revelations* by the Beato de Liébana and the 10th century *Emilian Codex*. Dating from the same period, the *Virgilian* or *Albeld Codex* has 99 illuminations. The German *Gospel* or *Golden Codex* has numerous exquisite illustrations and was made in the eleventh century for the emperors Conrad II and Henry II.

The thirteenth century is represented by *The Apocalypse* of the House of Savoy, Alfonso X The Wise's *Book of Dice* and two codices of his *Canticles* with a wealth of iconographic material relating to this period. The *Trojan Chronicle* is from the fourteenth century. A Flemish Book of Hours dates from the fifteenth century and contains miniatures on every page attributed to Gerard David. Among the Italian Renaissance manuscripts, the *Virgilian Codex* is outstanding. Lastly, special mention should be made of the *Antiquities* by the Portuguese Francisco de Holanda.

Artist known as the «Anónimo de la Cámara Regia»

Alfonso the Wise presiding over the game of chess according to Astronomy.

Book of the Games of Chess, Dice and Trick-track of King Alfonso X The Wise.

Illuminated manuscript, parchment. Hispano-French School, 1283.

Royal Library.

The Palace

The King's Oratory, beneath the cenotaph of Philip II, connecting the Main Chapel of the Basilica with the King's Chamber.

The Portrait or Audience Room. King's Quarters, King's House: dado of Talavera Renaissance tiles, 1570-73 made by Juan Fernández; German inlaid marquetry door, 1568; series of portraits of Habsburg monarchs; Chinese folding chairs, Ming Dynasty, c. 1570.

THE KING'S HOUSE

The palace complex is subdivided into two areas: the public or administrative area and the residential one. The first is similar in form to the core of the main cloister whereas the latter, the King's House, constitutes "the grill handle", linked to the chancel of the Church. This house has a clear form and structure as an addition to the main building while the administrative building is totally devoid of any distinguishing features.

Access to the royal rooms is through a narrow section which forms a link with the rest of the building. These rooms are configured as interdependent units, devoid of any attempt to emphasise the royal space. According to Kubler, the role of El Escorial as a palace was its least prominent function, as this was limited to providing the necessary facilities to accommodate the royal family, their servants and the immediate members of the court. A restrained style of architecture was therefore designed to reflect these functional limitations. As Bustamante García noted, it is highly significant that there is no large doorway to the palace complex like those at the entrances to the school and the monastery.

The so-called Public or Administrative Palace is actually closer to the second of these descriptions, as it lacks a courtly or palatial atmosphere. The northern and eastern walls of the façades were commissioned in 1573-74. This simple but grand complex was dubbed "the monastery of unfrocked monks" by Father Sigüenza and its centre is the Palace or Carriage Courtyard, magnificently articulated with plain pilasters and corridors as wide as those in the opposite cloister. However, on the western side of the courtyard, the T-shaped kitchens encroach up to the level of the ground floor. The vaulting in this area was realised at the beginning of the 1580s. The courtyard is thus divided into two, with this type of unsatisfactory improvised solution arising from the difficulty of adapting the building's new needs to the rigidity of the "universal design".

Two series of battle scenes depicting events from the reign of Philip II hang on the walls of the eastern and southern galleries. One of the series is Flemish and dates from the seventeenth century. Its subject is *The Campaign in the Low Countries*. The other by Luca Cambiaso represents *The victory at Lepanto*.

Don Álvaro de Luna, Constable of Castile, before his troops in battle order Detail of *The Battle of La Higueruela*.
Fresco on the south wall, 1584-90.
Hall of Battles.
King's House.

The Hall of Battles links the public palace with the King's House. Splendidly decorated in fresco with a programme intended to exalt the struggle against the French and Islam, there are serious doubts about its original function. If it was a place for ceremonies, it does not fit into any logical sequence. Bury suggested that it was a kind of winter walkway similar to those which existed in France in the late Middle Ages and later adopted in England and Italy. If that were the case, it is surprising that these modest although elegant rooms with their intimate domestic function had such ornate decoration and a use of symbolism more appropriate to the regal display found in other interiors in the Monastery.

The area designated by Juan de Herrera as the Private Royal Gallery has a standard official appearance but, in contrast to other *piezas largas* (long rooms) from this period, it does not seem to have been used for solemn receptions. According

Hall of Battles. King's House.

Niccolò Granello, Fabrizio Castello, Lazzaro Tavarone and Orazio Cambiaso

Wall and ceiling frescoes, 1584-90.

Niccolò Granello, Fabrizio Castello, Lazzaro Tavarone and Orazio Cambiaso
Clash between the Christian Forces and the Muslims. Detail from *The Battle of La Higueruela*.
Fresco on the south wall, 1584-90. Hall of Battles. King's House.

to Bustamante, it is highly significant that the largest and most luxurious hall in the palace did not form part of a public area but, instead, belonged to the King's private rooms.

This vast gallery is 55 metres long, 6 metres wide and 8 metres high at the highest point of the hemispherical vault with its small lunettes. Its decoration dates between 1584 and at least 1590 and was executed by Niccolò Granello, Fabrizio Castello, Lazzaro Tavarone and Orazio Cambiaso, the latter in charge of this group of artists. On the immense wall opposite the windows is *The Battle of Higueruel,* a combat won by John II in 1431 against the inhabitants of Granada according to an old grisaille in the Alcázar in Segovia.

On the balcony walls and the end walls is a commemoration of the triumph of the reigning sovereign over his French opponents. Whereas the balcony walls show the war of 1557-58, including four episodes from the victory of Saint Quentin, the end ones show the successful and then still recent operations in the Azores in 1582-83. It is therefore evident that, in relation to the struggle for supremacy in Europe, the iconographic programme suggests an ideological continuity between the medieval crusade against the Moors and the modern one against the Turks. However, the message became so unclear due to the profusion of anecdotal details that, a short after its execution, Father Sigüenza was unable to identify some episodes correctly.

The scenes simulate tapestries in a reference not so much to the most typical and courtly manner of covering walls, but rather to series such as *The Conquest of Tunisia.* This constituted an emblematic allusion to the man who represented the archetypal hero in the eyes of Philip II: his father Charles V.

(Left)
The Capture of Santa Fe, detail of *The Battle of La Higueruela,* on the south wall.
(Right)
Expedition of Philip II to the Island of Tercera (The Azores), on the west wall.
Fresco in the Hall of Battles.
1584-90.
King's House.

For Brown the programme here, within the context of a building largely decorated with religious art, could be explained in terms of a divine mission. Following the example of the Emperor, the King inherited the responsibility attached to the role of defender of the faith. In fact, the paintings in the Hall of Battles, like those in the library, do not require spiritual explanations, as they are outside the sacred realm: the Escorial is not only a monastery.

The organisation of the subjects seems to tie in with the purpose that Bury ascribed to the gallery. According to Brown, "the frescoes were meant to be contemplated during a stroll up and down, although we still do not know who could have been the person invited to take a stroll."

In spite of its dominant position in the El Escorial complex, close to the high altar end of the basilica and closely linked to the main chapel, the King's House or residential part of the palace building is relatively small and unpretentious. Holy and isolated in these remote rooms "where no-one else can go without permission, like eagles in the inaccessible peaks", this is where we find Philip II, the instrument of divine providence but also the protector of the Church and ultimately the mediator between the sacred and the secular. Over and above its small size and modest appearance, the King's House constitutes the focal point of the whole structure and the final link in a chain made up of numerous elements.

Although this tentacle-like projection of the grill handle is well-known, it cannot be clearly appreciated from the inside of the vast monastery-fortress. As Bustamante pointed out, the area of the monarch's private rooms is a separate world: deliberately isolated, unattainable, and without a direct entrance. It was one of the zones that Juan Bautista de Toledo lavished most attention on and it was never subjected to any alteration after the production of the 1562 "universal design".

As with many other parts of El Escorial, the building history is somewhat confused. By 1564, Juan Bautista de Toledo had already designed the Royal House. According to Bustamante, by the time of Toledo's death three years later, progress had been made as far as ground level in the Courtyard of the

The Prior's Tower and the King's Private Garden from the windows of the King's Ante-chamber. King's House.

The Oratory of Philip II, which connects the Main
Chapel of the Basilica with the King's Bedroom.
TITIAN
Christ on the Route to Calvary (copy).
The King's Room. The King's Quarters.

ESCORIAL WORKSHOP
Holy water bucket and sprinkler. Cast,
chased and gilt-bronze, late 16th-century.
Chamber of Philip II. The King's Quarters.
King's House.

JUAN DE HERRERA
Chimney pot of ridged
design with top, roof of the
Courtyard of the Masks.

Masks complex, which linked up the grill handle. Kubler dated the start of the project to 1570-72, at the time of work on the end wall of the church but Bustamante states that the work was carried out entirely in that two-year period. Records show that the rooms had been completed by 1581 but the sovereign did not begin to use them until five years later.

For its simplicity, size, location and overall concept, the private palace derives from a particular type of architecture. For Bustamante, it was envisaged as a country house or retreat, a villa or *belvedere*, merging with the garden and the kitchen garden, and therefore without a façade.

The Courtyard of Masks, overshadowed by the enormous wall of the church, owes its name to the two fountains on its eastern side. On the lower level of its other three sides it has three respective gateways with semi-circular arches on Tuscan columns, the architectural order appropriate for a country residence. In contrast to such an Italianate style, the roofs and the curious chimney tops provide a picturesque Flemish touch. These date from the time when El Escorial was founded, since only the roofs in this section survived the dreadful fire of 1671 intact.

Around what Herrera described as "the courtyard of the Royal Residence" is the monarch's house, on two levels, with its summer rooms on the ground floor and winter rooms on the first or main floor. As well as this seasonal distinction, there is another characteristic feature of the Spanish royal tradition comprising two rooms of similar layout, one for the King and the other the Queen. Here, the rooms are placed in such a way that the altar of the basilica can be seen from each bedroom through the prayer grill: "Thus the king and queen are inside (so to speak) and outside the High Altar; this could not have been more appropriately or magnificently designed."

The Queen's Quarter, also called the Infanta's Quarter is on the north side and corresponds to the main or Gospel side of the church. It was used by princess Isabel Clara Eugenia, hence the alternative name of the room, after her father was left as a widower for the fourth and last time in 1580.

The austerity of these rooms stems from their function as a pious retreat. This governed the way in which the royal residence was incorpo-

The Queen's or Infanta's Chamber.
Main room with doorways, Bedroom and Study.

Portable organ. Detail of the keyboard inlaid with ivory and ebony, with the carved arms of Philip II on the front in Renaissance style, Flemish workshop, 16th-century.
Queen's Quarter.
King's House.

King's Chamber.
The main room, with the
doorways to the Study and
the Bedroom of Philip II,
and cupboard with the
Monastery's Talavera
ceramics, small works of art
and objects.
King's Quarter.
King's House.

rated into the Hieronymite monastery, following the old model of a palace-monastery. Although this austerity is excessive for a country house, it is counterbalanced by important works of art which help to create the current atmosphere. The very fact that these rooms are hidden away expresses this feeling of asceticism, averse not to magnificence and any from of outward show, although conforming to the requirements imposed by etiquette. According to Von der Osten Sacken, the labyrinthine approach was part of traditional Burgundian court ritual and it seems likely that these additional difficulties of access made the monarch increasingly inaccessible, locked in a system of rigid demarcations based on rooms and ranks. Protocol determined how far the visitor could get, depending on his position in the hierarchy.

Within the Queen's Quarter, which looks out onto a garden of the same name, is the Infanta's Chamber with a portrait of Isabel Clara Eugenia, attributed by some to Bartolomé González but tentatively by other scholars to Pantoja de la Cruz. The portrait of her sister, the Infanta Catalina

Canopied bed. Walnut wood with Flemish tapestry.

Bedroom within the Room of Philip II.

King's Quarters.

King's House.

JUAN PANTOJA DE LA CRUZ
The Elderly Charles V in Armour, 1599.
Copy of a lost original by Titian.
Portrait Room or Audience Room.
King's Quarters.
King's House.

Micaela, can more confidently be ascribed to Pantoja. Both portraits are based on paintings by Alonso Sánchez Coello (1585-88 and around 1584, respectively) now in the Prado. The small hand-organ has Philip II's coat of arms on the front and is of Flemish manufacture.

Behind the High Altar end of the church, The King's Chamber connects with that of the Queen. The dado with its decorative Talavera tiles is the original one. The Anteroom has paintings by Juan Correa de Vivar and the workshop of the Bassano. *The Adoration of The Shepherds, The Crowning with Thorns* and *The Supper at Emmaus* are by a follower of Bassano, according to Arslan, however, the painting that completes the series, a *Noli me tangere,* is in fairly good condition and in the opinion of Ruiz Gómez is a work of unquestionable quality and fluent brush-strokes. With small variants, it follows a preliminary study attributed to Jacopo Bassano. Here, we see the sedan chair used by Philip II during the last few years of his life when he was suffering from gout. It could be converted into a bed through an ingenious system by which the back was let down and locked into place. The King used the chair for his last journey to El Escorial.

Now known as The Portrait Room, The Audience Room was used for routine receptions. Philip II used the Chinese, Ming-dynasty (ca. 1570) folding chairs to rest his gouty foot. On the walls are important portraits of Habsburg monarchs.

The portrait of the elderly *Charles V* in armour is signed by Pantoja de la Cruz in 1579. However, it also bears a second inscription with the date of 1547, as it is a copy of a magnificent original by Titian, which was lost in the fire at the palace of El Pardo. The Emperor is depicted more than half-length and is holding a baton of office with his feathered helmet on a table. The attributes here are confined to military ones, but the painting is still a symbol of monarchical power. The portrait of *Philip II* shows him in half-armour in a coat of mail and, like Charles V, holding a baton of office in his right hand. This splendid work by Anton Van Dashorst Mor (known in Spain as Antonio Moro) was painted in 1557, the year of the battle of San Quintín. The victor thus wears the same attire that he wore at the scene of his triumph.

Bartolomé González
Philip IV as a Child in Armour, 1612.
Portrait Room or Audience Room.
King's Quarters.
King's House.

Juan Pantoja de la Cruz
Don Juan de Austria, copy of an
original by Alonso Sánchez Coello.
Portrait Room or Audience Room.
King's Quarters.
King's House.

Galería de Paseo, from the
north wall.
ABRAHAM ORTELIUS
Series of engravings of maps
from the *Theatrum Orbis
Terrarum,* 16th-century.
Series of paintings on canvas
of Philip II's military
campaigns.

While Philip II did not share Charles V's passion for war, he had a similar liking for heroic imagery. As Checa Cremades has pointed out, this is one of the first uses of the distanced, aloof image of Philip II which he strove with such effort to project in court circles. The severity of the face, the strong highlights on the armour and the imprecise, neutral background all serve to individualise the portrait, even psychologically, within a sub-genre which from then on would be codified as a new type for the representation of the monarch.

The series is completed with portraits of *Philip IV* as a child signed by Bartolomé González in 1612, and of *Charles II,* by Carreño de Miranda dating from about 1675-76. The other portraits are also of members of the Habsburg dynasty. Two outstanding works are the portrait of Juana of Austria, attributed to Sánchez Coello, and that of Juan of Austria, a copy of an original by Sánchez Coello by Pantoja de la Cruz.

ESCORIAL WORKSHOP.
Desk set of two inkwells
and sand-box.
Engraved and gilt-bronze,
late 16th-century.
Chamber of Philip II.
King's Quarters.
King's House.

Connecting with the Galería del Paseo and through this with the King's Hall are pairs of marquetry-inlaid doors "the best and finest-made to have come from Germany, well-designed and

GERMAN WORKSHOP, Augsburg, 1562-68: monumental doorway.
Maple, walnut, beech and pear wood with ebony veneer. Inlaid marquetry with architectural
and geometric motifs based on prints by Hans Vredeman de Vries. Doorway between the
Ante-chamber or King's Room and the Galería del Paseo. King's Quarters. King's House.

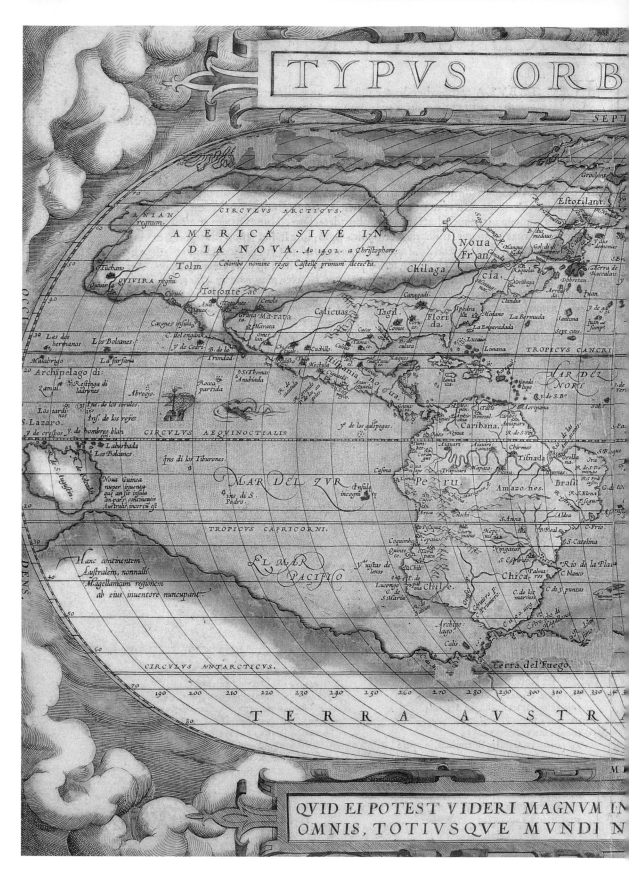

ABRAHAM ORTELIUS

Map of the Earth, from the *Theatrum Orbis Terrarum*. Coloured engraving, 16th-century.

Galería de Paseo. King's Quarters. King's House.

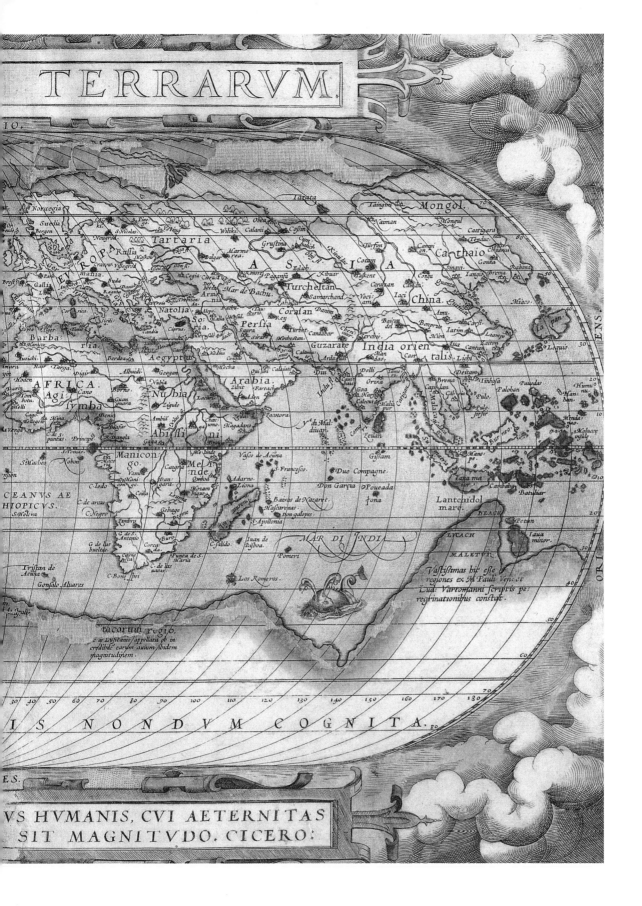

TERRARVM.

10.

IS NONDVM COGNITA. 80

VS HVMANIS, CVI AETERNITAS
SIT MAGNITVDO. CICERO:

MADRID SCHOOL, 17ᵀᴴ-century
Series of the Royal Houses
around Madrid.
(Above) *View of the Royal
Palace of Valsaín.*
(Below) *View of the Royal
Residence of El Pardo.*
Ante-chamber of Philip II.
King's Quarter.
King's House.

conceived." These were a gift from the Emperor Maximilian II. The Galería del Paseo is 35 metres long and typologically is a simpler version of the Hall of Battles. In earlier reconstructions, it was mistakenly thought to be a throne room. Although Von der Osten Sacken was aware of the room's earlier decorative function, he not only identified it as a large audience chamber, here but also analyses the iconography of the set of tapestries used as a canopy over the supposed throne as if the room had really been used for this purpose.

The Galería was redecorated according to Father Sigüenza's descriptive references and today displays engravings of maps by the famous fifteenth-century geographer Abraham Ortelius. Replacing the Flemish landscapes hung here by Philip II are canvases of contemporary battles. The Jesuit Juan Wedlingen was responsible for installing the meridian lines on the floor in this room and the next one in 1755.

Parallel with the Galería del Paseo, two inner rooms look out on-

to the Courtyard of the Masks and are hung with 16ᵗʰ- and 17ᵗʰ-century paintings. *The Virgin and Child* by Quintín Metsys is an outstanding work, as is *The Moneychanger and his Wife* by Marinus Van Reymerswade, signed and dated 1538. Like the Prado version, which was painted a year later and is slightly different, it derives from a subject developed by the Master of Louvain.

The King's Hall or Anteroom features a well-known series of paintings of Philip IV's residences near Madrid with provide us with a fairly complete idea of the network of residences established by his grandfather. In 1630, the King commissioned Jusepe Leonardo, Félix Castelló, Juan de la Corte and Pedro Núñez with these works. They represent country estates such as El Prado, Aranjuez and Valsaín painted in a detailed, descriptive style which makes them a source of valuable historical information. However, it is very difficult to clarify who painted which scene.

The foreground views of the palaces of Valsaín and Aranjuez have a markedly architectural dimension, to the extent that the second does not depict the building as actually built but rather the project for it. By contrast, the view of El Pardo shows animated figures dotted about the broad foreground area (there is another version with variations in the Instituto Valencia de Don Juan, Madrid). The most outstanding view in the series is undoubtedly that of the house of Aceca by Jusepe Leonardo. Here, the figures are painted in a conventional Velázquian style with loose brush-strokes.

During the reign of Philip II this room was hung with a series of prints of El Escorial engraved by Pedro Perret and based on designs by Juan de Herrera. Some of these prints have been reincorporated into the decoration of this room which was also originally hung with "pictures of many objects that can be seen in our Indies, painted in their natural condition", the result of the huge collecting endeavour on the part of the royal doctor, Francisco Hernández.

Passing along a corridor on one side of the King's Staircase, the route leads to Philip II's chamber, with splendid views to the east and to the south, undoubtedly the best in the whole building. The furniture has been arranged in an attempt to recreate the atmosphere of Philip's last hours, as it was here that he died on September 13 1598 "... in the very house and church of Saint Lawrence that he had built, almost above his own tomb, at five o'clock in the morning while dawn was breaking in the east ... when the children from the seminary were singing the early morning mass, the last one said for his life and the first for his death..." however, some works which so well summarise Philip's devotional style, for example, Bosch's *Table of the Deadly Sins,* now in the Prado, cannot be returned, so the present setting is really more of a simple evocation.

(Above) HANS DE EVALO
Portable clock with lamp.
Chased and gilt-bronze,
silver and steel, Madrid, 1583.
Study of the King's Chamber.
(Below) GIULIANO DELLA
PORTA
Altarpiece with the Calvary,
by Antonio Gentili. Ebony,
silver and gilt-bronze,
c. 1570-85.
Chamber of Philip II.
King's Quarters.
King's House.

LIMOGES WORKSHOP, France, c. 1200-10. Casket-reliquary. Scenes of the martyrdom of the Archbishop of Canterbury, Saint Thomas à Beckett, instigated by King Henry II Plantaganet in 1170, and the Burial of the Archbishop. Oak, engraved, gilded and relief-enamelled copper plaquettes. Chamber of Philip II. King's Quarters. King's House.

Following the design pioneered at Yuste, the King could turn from his bed towards splendid views of the landscape, as well as towards his oratory and the High Altar of the basilica. An important bronze clock can be seen on the writing desk, with a female figure holding up the dial. This characteristic Mannerist object – as much a valuable historical memento as a work of art - was made in Madrid and signed in 1583 by Hans de Evalo, Philip II's Royal Watchmaker. According to the famous account by Jean Lhermite, this was one of two clocks used by King, this one only marking the hours. When the monarch wrote at night, the only illumination came from a small lamp, lit next to the face of the clock.

Notable among the mainly Flemish and Italian 16th-century religious paintings are a *Sacra conversazione* or *Virgin and Child between Saint Roch and Saint Sebastian* by Benvenuto Tisi, il Garafalo, a *Pietà* by Gerard David, and a portrait of the elderly Philip II by Pantoja de la Cruz.

More interesting is a remarkable panel by the Flemish artist Vrancke van der Stockt, a pupil of Van der Weyden and the official painter to the city of Brussels following the death of his master in 1464. The central theme on the front of the panel is *The Presentation of the Virgin in the Temple,* accompanied by other scenes from her life depicted on either side beneath small canopies. *Mary Magdalen* and *Saint Nicholas* are depicted on the reverse. With its brilliant chromatic range, Friedländer associated this work with the *Cambrai Altarpiece* in the Prado which was Van der Stockt's masterpiece according to Bermejo Martínez.

The ebony, silver and bronze altar in this room was made in Rome by Antonio Gentili after a design by Giuliano della Porta, and was presented by the Grand Duchess of Tuscany to Philip II as a gift in 1586. In the cabinet are other precious objects such as two small boxes, one made of bone in the tenth century and the other a 12th-century Limoges enamel casket in the Romanesque style. A Plateresque silver pix made in the shape of a church by the famous silversmith Luis del Castillo dates from the 16th century. Two paintings on agate attributed to Annibale Carracci date from the end of that century.

French Gothic art, 14th century: Diptych of Queen Juana of Castile, with scenes from the Life of Christ.

Carved and polychrome ivory in high relief.

Chamber of Philip II. King's Quarters. King's House.

FELIPE DE SILVA

Allegory of Philip V defeating Heresy, c. 1707-12.

The King is accompanied by Faith, killing a dragon, opposite
his first wife, Maria Luisa Gabriela of Savoy and the Prince
of Asturias, Don Luis; in the background is the Monastery of
El Escorial with the Virgin as Protector, surrounded by angels
between Saint Jerome and Saint Lawrence, in the sky.
Juan de Villanueva's staircase.
Palace of the Bourbons.

THE PALACE OF THE BOURBONS

Charles III, like his predecessors, continued to occupy the King's House or *grill handle*. He also ordered the remodelling of the eastern and northern wings of the so-called Public or Administrative Palace, used under the Habsburgs by the Infantes and most important courtiers, in order to accommodate his family, particularly the Princes of Asturias. It was in fact Charles IV who took this change further by deciding to continue to use the same rooms that he had occupied while still heir to the throne.

He thus undertook the necessary work, not only involving redecoration but also architectural redesign, with the aim of making this area a true royal palace. The problem dating from the time of construction of suitable access was solved by Juan de Villanueva in 1793 through alterations to the northern façade and the construction of a new staircase, an exercise in virtuosity that took maximum visual advantage of its evident narrowness.

The coherence of planning and decoration, the relatively well-preserved original layout, and the richness of its tapestries from the Royal Manufactory of Santa Barbara, Madrid make this the most characteristic of Spanish Bourbon palaces. A number of tapestry series were expressly commissioned for the building depending on the potential use of certain rooms. In 1775 and 1791-92, Goya painted various series of sketches and cartoons for use in the preparation of these tapestries. On other occasions pre-made

Door between the Hall of Battles in the King's House and the Ante-chamber of the Queen's Quarters in the Palace of the Bourbons.

tapestries were used, although so well installed that they appear to have been made expressly for that location. In 1789, after his ascent to the throne, Charles IV, little interested in El Pardo, location of 'la jornada de invierno' (the winter stay), removed the tapestries from that palace and installed them in El Escorial, which was used for *La jornada de otoño* (the autumn stay).

Both at the favoured Escorial and at El Pardo, the tapestry had a clear function as a protection against the cold. This need may also have given rise to the compartmentalization of space by means of small rooms. The autumn residence consists of a succession of spaces where the striking colours of the tapestries, the furniture in white and gilt wood or mahogany with bronze mounts, and the numerous and attractive ceil-

Pompeiian Room. Palace of the Bourbons.

Furniture from the period of Ferdinand VII. Tapestries from the Madrid Royal Tapestry

Manufactory based on preparatory cartoons by Agustín and Juan Navarro.

The Ambassadors' Ante-room. Palace of the Bourbons.

Neo-classical furniture. Tapestries from the Madrid Royal Tapestry Manufactory, 1778-80,

after preparatory cartoons by Francisco de Goya.

The Pots and Pans Seller and *The Maja and the cloaked Men* (Above) *Card Players, The Washerwomen*

and *The Kite* (Below).

The Ambassadors' Room. Palace of the Bourbons. Furniture from the period of Ferdinand VII. Tapestries from the Madrid Royal Tapestry Manufactory, after preparatory cartoons by Francisco and Ramón Bayeu. *Children playing at bullfighting, The Mule Driver and The Gardener, The Game of Bowls,* and *The Sausage Seller Pedro Rico.*

Popular types with a Dog. Tapestry from the Madrid Royal Tapestry Manufactory, after a preparatory cartoon by Goya.

ings by Felipe López create a warm and welcoming mood, the antithesis of the building founded by Philip II.

Although the atmosphere of the period is maintained, the fact that many of the tapestries came from elsewhere, as well as the alterations to which they were subjected until the beginning of the nineteenth century, make it difficult for us to interpret them correctly as integrated elements in a unified decorative programme commissioned for specific rooms and based on preparatory cartoons by specific artists.

The upper landing of the staircase leads to the King's Room through the three westernmost small rooms on the northern side where Charles IV's workshops were situated. Notable here are several religious paintings by Mariano Salvador Maella and three pieces of biscuit porcelain from the Naples Royal Manufactory, decorated with portraits of the corre-

Private Dining Room. Palace of the Bourbons.

Neo-classical furniture. Tapestries from the Madrid Royal Tapestry Manufactory

after preparatory cartoons by Andrés Ginés de Aguirre.

The Game of Pelota and *Cibeles and the Puerta de Alcalá*.

Madrid Royal Tapestry
Manufactory
(Above) *Cibeles and the
Puerta de Alcalá,* after a
preparatory cartoon by
Andrés Ginés de Aguirre.
Private Dining Room.
(Abajo) *The Paseo de las
Delicias* in Madrid, detail,
after a preparatory cartoon
by Ramón Bayeu. The
Ceremonial Dining Room.
Palace of the Bourbons.

Madrid Royal Tapestry
Manufactory.
(Above)
*Ladies feeding the Ducks in
the Pond of the Buen Retiro*
after a preparatory cartoon
by José del Castillo.
The King's Oratory.
(Abajo)
*A Stroll by the Statues in the
Garden of the Buen Retiro,*
after a preparatory cartoon
by José del Castillo.
King's Room, former
Bedroom of the Infantas'
Quarters.
Palace of the Bourbons.

Madrid Royal Tapestry Manufactory.

Ladies and Gentlemen out strolling, after a preparatory cartoon by José del Castillo.

The King's Bedroom. Palace of the Bourbons.

sponding branch of the Bourbon family. The China Cabinet Room derives its name from a display-case in the Neo-classical style. In keeping with its original function, it now displays an English service from the Copeland factory, a wedding present from George V to Alfonso XIII and Victoria Eugenia.

The Grand Dining Room, a former billiards room, was the first to be hung with tapestries, here based on cartoons by Goya such as *The Woodcutters* and *The Dance on the Banks of the Manzanares*. There are also cartoons by Bayeu and Castillo. In the next area, serving as a vestibule to the Villanueva Staircase, hang tapestries based on designs by Anglois, Antonio González Velázquez and Calleja based on compositions by Teniers and Wouwerman. Those in the anteroom are after Bayeu and Goya, the latter represented by such well-known compositions as *The Maja and the cloaked Men, The Kite* and *The Pots and Pans Seller*. In The Ambassadors' Room with its painted ceiling by Felipe López are further tapestries after compositions by Bayeu such as *Pedro Rico, the Sausage Seller*. The altar in the King's Oratory has a *Holy Family* by Luca Giordano.

The Audience Room. Palace of the Bourbons. Neo-Gothic furniture, 1832. Tapestries from the Madrid Royal Tapestry Manufactory. *Boar hunting, Flower Urns or Spring,* and *The Soldier and the Young Lady,* based on preparatory cartoons by Francisco de Goya. *The Picnic,* based on a preparatory cartoon by Ramón Bayeu.

The Infantas' Recreation Room. Palace of the Bourbons. Furniture from the period of Ferdinand VII. Brussels tapestries, 1729-45, woven by Daniel and Urbano Leyniers, after cartoons by Jan van Orley. *Venus sends Cupid to arouse Telemachus of desires, Calypso tries to discover Mentor's secret,* and *Venus asks Neptune to destroy Telemachus' Ship,* from the series of *The Adventures of Telemachus.*

In the Infantas' Rooms, the room traditionally known as The Recreation Room is today called The Telemachus Room after the young hero whose adventures are depicted by Leyniers in an early 18th-century Brussels tapestry. From the bedroom onwards, the tapestries are once again from the Madrid factory, here based on cartoons by Bayeu and Aguirre. The nursemaids' room is called the Pompeiian Room on account of the motifs on the brilliant decorative tapestries, the work of Agustín and Juan Navarro which have large medallions like cameos. The hall is decorated with tapestries based on cartoons by Goya, Castillo and Bayeu.

In the Queen's Rooms, the Ushers' Room has hunting scenes based on designs by Goya, Castillo and Aguirre while those in the hallway leading to the Queen's Rooms, a space directly linked with the Hall of Battles, are after Teniers. The Room of the Queen's Retinue has tapestries after Bayeu, Goya and Castillo, magnificent console tables made during the reign of Charles IV and, in the centre, an English piano from the beginning of the nineteenth century made by Thomas Tomkinson. This room leads to

Brussels Tapestry, 1729-45, woven by Daniel and Urbano Leyniers
after a cartoon by Jan van Orley.

Venus asks Neptune to destroy Telemachus' Ship (detail), from the series of
The Adventures of Telemachus.

The Infantas' Recreation Room. Palace of the Bourbons.

Oval Room. King's Quarter. Palace of the Bourbons. (Rigth) Pompeiian style tapestries, 1780-90. Madrid Royal Tapestry Manufactory, after preparatory cartoons by José del Castillo.
(Left) Naples Royal Manufactory: casket with allegories of *The Forces of Love and Evil*. Soft-paste porcelain and gilt-bronze, 1780-85.
(Below) The King's Oratory. The King's Quarter. Palace of the Bourbons. Altar with the *Holy Family* by Luca Giordano.

the Oratory, with its Neo-classical objects including the silver-gilt candelabra made at the Martínez Royal Madrid Factory. Scenes by Goya, Aguirre and Castillo decorate the former Dressing Room, now known as the everyday Dining Room.

The room now called the King's Bedroom has a splendid bed made in France in the transitional style between Neo-classical and the Empire style of Charles IV. The Bathroom is furnished in the style fashionable during the reign of Ferdinand with tapestries on the walls based on cartoons by Castillo and Aguirre among others. An interesting space with Neo-classical wall decoration houses the lavatory. The room now called the Queen's Bedroom has tapestries with views of Madrid designed by Aguirre. Exceptionally, the Sewing Room still has its original collection of tapestries with Pompeiian motifs based on cartoons by Castillo made to furnish this "oval room" of the then Princess of Asturias, María Luisa de Parma. The Audience Room is decorated with scenes by Goya, Bayeu and Castillo under a ceiling by Felipe López and is furnished with an early Neo-Gothic suite dating from the reign of Ferdinand VII and made by the cabinetmaker Ángel Maeso in 1832.

The King's Bedroom. Palace of the Bourbons.

Furniture in the transitional style between Neo-classical and Empire.

Tapestries and carpet from Madrid Royal Tapestry Manufactory.

Tropical hardwood rooms,
1793-1815.
Palace of the Bourbons.
Oratory (Left)
The King's Study (Right)

From here we move on to the rooms decorated with tropical hardwoods. These reveal the very high standards attained in cabinet-making and the decorative arts during the reigns of Charles IV and Ferdinand VII. These four rooms – the Office, the Lavatory, the Ante-oratory and the Oratory - were all decorated with marquetry using tropical hardwoods from the Indies. Work began in 1793 and was resumed in 1815, reaching completion until 1831.

Their unified decorative scheme is derived from a wide variety of classical sources. Conventional Pompeiian forms alternate with direct borrowings from the repertoire employed by Robert Adam and other European decorators at the end of the eighteenth century. In the Office, the most lavishly decorated area, is a magnificent table decorated with reliefs of historical events such as the Surrender of Granada. During the reign of Ferdinand VII, Angel Maeso was chiefly responsible for this decorative project.

Dado panel (detail).

ROYAL WORKSHOPS (before 1843): wall border in embroidered silk. ÁNGEL MAESO: inlaid marquetry in tropical hardwoods.

BARTOLOMÉ MONTALVO: oils on copper. IGNACIO MILLÁN: : chased and gilt bronzes.

The King's Study. Tropical hardwood rooms, 1793-1815. Palace of the Bourbons.

New museums

(Above)
Reproduction of the crane used to move the blocks. Machines Gallery.

(Below)
Model of the structure of the spire of a tower. Carpentry Gallery. Architecture Museum.

(Previous page)
Original bricklayers' and masons' tools used in the construction of the Monastery. Tools Gallery. Architecture Museum.

THE MUSEUM OF ARCHITECTURE

The major restoration programme of 1963 involved refurbishing a part of what Herrera referred to as "the floor with vaults", giving it a purely didactic function. These rooms could now be accessed from the two introductory rooms of the Paintings Museum in the Palace or Carriage Courtyard. Recently improved for exhibitions held in 1986, the Museum of Architecture is a didactic display with plans, scale models and other objects that illustrate the construction process at El Escorial. The display features some of the original workmen's tools.

THE MUSEUM OF ART

As part of the major restoration programme started in 1963, a decision was taken to exhibit the paintings still in the monastery (with the exception of the fixed decorative cycles) according to modern museological criteria. As introductory rooms, two 16th-century grand rooms in the Public or Administrative Palace which been partitioned off and radically altered in the eighteenth century were opened up again. The ground floor of the King's House, namely the Summer Palace, was restored and equipped to house the main part of the collection.

The entrance to the two museum buildings is located outside the itinerary in the centre of the eastern corridor of the Palace or Carriage Courtyard. The first hall contains the polychrome wood sculpture of *Saint Michael Triumphant over Lucifer,* made for El Escorial at the request of Charles II by Luisa Roldán, "la Roldana", in 1692, the year of her appointment as Royal Sculptor. The post did not, however, include remuneration. This is her most renowned work and almost the only one in this typically Spanish technique within the international artistic context of the palace-monastery.

According to Martín González, Luisa Roldán was able to successfully pass this test, a decisive one for her future. A notable artist of small-scale works, she sculpted the Saint Michael, presented as a victorious Archangel, larger than life-size in keeping with the intended location. Using a palette of strong but flat colours, the work is adapted in tone and spirit to the official context of the Monastery.

These two halls are decorated by several Flemish tapestries from the collection assembled by Philip II. The most outstanding among these are the famous series entitled the *Triumph of the Mother of God,* known as *The Golden Tapestries (Paños de Oro),* and the series called the *Canopy of Charles V.* Also on show are two further tapestries belonging to Margarita of Austria, *Christ bearing the Cross* and *The Crucifixion,* and the *Hieronymous Bosch Series,* based on paintings by the artist.

The Salón de Honor in the museum had the same function in the Public or Administrative Palace. The most important painting currently

LUISA ROLDÁN
"LA ROLDANA"
*Saint Michael triumphant
over Lucifer,* 1692.
Carved, polychrome and
gilded wood.
Ante-room of Honour.
Public Palace.

MANUFACTORY OF PIERRE VAN DER AELST (active 1495-1531), Brussels.

Woven from the Devotion of Our Lady series known as the «Golden Tapestries»,

woven for Queen Juana of Castile. Gold, silver, silk and wool thread, c. 1502-04.

(Above) *God sends the Archangel Gabriel to the Virgin Mary,* Ante-room of Honour.

(Below) *The Annunciation.* Room of Honour.

Public Palace.

housed in the building is displayed here: *The Martyrdom of Saint Maurice and the Theban Legion* by El Greco. The painting was commissioned for one of the altars in the church in 1580 and El Greco began work in the same year, completing it two years later. Although Philip II paid handsomely for the painting, he declined to hang it up. Furthermore, in 1584, he replaced it with a version of the same story by Romolo Cincinnato.

Copious column inches have been devoted to this division of opinion between El Greco and the King. According to Father Sigüenza, "the picture of Saint Maurice and his soldiers did not please His Majesty (that does not mean too much), because it pleases few people, although it is said that it is very artistic and that the painter knows a lot and excellent things from his hand can be seen." Bypassing these initial reservations, Friar Francisco de Los Santos wrote in his *Descripción* of El Escorial in 1657 that he considered the painting to be "an admirable work, excellent and very artistic".

EL GRECO
(DOMENIKOS
THEOTOKOPOULOS)
The Martyrdom of Saint Maurice and the Theban Legion (detail).

Mulcahy endeavoured to prove that the canvas was rejected not for aesthetic reasons, but because it was iconographically unacceptable, as although Philip II may not have liked the style of the Cretan artist, he had very broad tastes and was capable of yielding, assuming that the contents were iconographically correct. Mulcahy's points have generally been accepted: the monarch dispensed with the painting because it failed to comply with Counter-Reformation requirements of decorum.

As Mulcahy points out, El Greco approached the subject intellectually, placing more emphasis on the decision to die than on death itself. According to Fernando Marías, he made a strong commitment to his art here, as indicated by his signature in the mouth of the serpent. This could represent wisdom or, equally, the satisfaction that comes from realising an outstanding achievement.

In the opinion of Camón Aznar, El Greco depicted himself in the second character to the right of the Saint, although Annie Cloulas and particularly John Bury have put forward a list of other possible identities for this figure including Manuel Filiberto of Savoy, Alessandro Farnese, Juan de Austria, and the Duke of Alba. Overall, El Greco imposed his own artistic preoccupations on this scene of martyrdom, which he conceived as a *sacra conversazione,* also using this opportunity to depict a portrait gallery of the most illustrious military leaders.

EL GRECO (DOMENIKOS THEOTOKOPOULOS)
The Martyrdom of Saint Maurice and the Theban Legion, 1580-83.
Room of Honour. Public Palace.

The choice of subject seems to have been influenced by the existence of a relic of this martyr saint in El Escorial. The iconography, based on "The Golden Legend", that tells the story of how Diocletian had Maurice and his companions killed for refusing to offer sacrifices to the pagan gods. Curiously, Cincinnato's canvas painting is a total tribute to El Greco's compositional solution, albeit within an ideological framework in strict conformance with Counter-Reformatory requirements.

In response to why El Greco was allowed to continue with his unsuitable proposal, Mulcahy has suggested that the King was absent in Portugal at the time the picture was being created. He further suggested that the terms of the commission were vague, thereby giving El Greco a false sense of artistic freedom. In spite of its removal from the basilica, the "picture portraying the story of Saint Maurice" acquired the status of a museum piece, emphasising Philip II's broad tastes. With this work of art, El Greco opened up to a more distinctive personalized form of expression from the starting point of his roots in the Venetian School and his admiration for Michelangelo.

In the former Summer Palace on the ground floor of the King's House, Room One contains a group of 16th-century Flemish paintings,

mainly by Michel Coxcie, the great Flemish artist whose style was deeply indebted to Roman work, expressed in a dignified interpretation of the art of Raphael and Leonardo da Vinci. Philip II particularly favoured Coxcie, who painted the *Saint Philip Altarpiece* in his honour. The central scene is the *Martyrdom of Saint Philip* with the *Preaching and Capture* of the saint on either side. Among other works by the artist here are the *Christ bearing the Cross* and *David and Goliath*. Works by other painters include the *Money-changer and his Wife* by Marinus Reymerswaele and an anonymous *Calvary*.

Flemish paintings are also displayed in Room Two, these dating from the 17th century. The most important of these is *Philip III's visit to San Sebastián* attributed to Paul van der Muelen. It depicts the monarch stopping at San Sebastián en route to the Isla de los Faisanes (Pheasant Island) to take part in the diplomatic pre-nuptial ceremony known as the "Handover of the Princesses", together with the French king. This is followed by a *Landscape with Peasants* by Jan Brueghel II the Younger and two still lifes, one by Joris van Son and the other by Peter Boel. There are also two copies after Van Dyck, a *Holy Family* and *The Virgin and Child,* as well as a pair of *Floral Still Lifes* by Daniel Seghers.

(Left)
DOMENICO TINTORETTO
Mary Magdalen.
First Room. Summer
Palace. King's House.
(Right)
PIETRO MARTIRE NERI
Pope Innocent X with a Prelate.
Fourth Room. Summer
Palace. King's House.

GIOVANNI FRANCESCO BARBIERI, "IL GUERCINO"

Lot made drunk by his Daughters.

Sixth Room. Summer Palace. King's House.

Michel Coxcie

David and Goliath.

Third Room. Summer Palace. King's House.

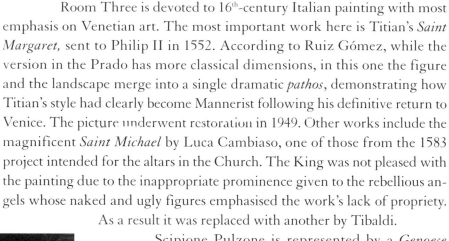

FEDERICO ZUCCARO
The Adoration of the Shepherds, 1588 (details). Seventh Room. Galería de Paseo. Summer Palace. King's House.

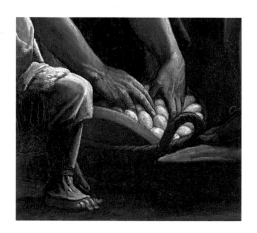

Room Three is devoted to 16th-century Italian painting with most emphasis on Venetian art. The most important work here is Titian's *Saint Margaret,* sent to Philip II in 1552. According to Ruiz Gómez, while the version in the Prado has more classical dimensions, in this one the figure and the landscape merge into a single dramatic *pathos,* demonstrating how Titian's style had clearly become Mannerist following his definitive return to Venice. The picture underwent restoration in 1949. Other works include the magnificent *Saint Michael* by Luca Cambiaso, one of those from the 1583 project intended for the altars in the Church. The King was not pleased with the painting due to the inappropriate prominence given to the rebellious angels whose naked and ugly figures emphasised the work's lack of propriety. As a result it was replaced with another by Tibaldi.

Scipione Pulzone is represented by a *Genoese Family,* while Palma Giovane was the author of *The Penitent Saint Jerome* and *Saint Francis in Ecstasy.* God the Father and the Holy Spirit is attributed to Paolo Veronese: although not included in the modern catalogues raisonné, Ruiz Gómez was confident of its attribution, considering that its high quality as well as the physical types confirm the authorship, also represented here by a *Descent from the Cross.* Another *Descent from the Cross* is by Veronese's son, Carlo Veronese, who follows compositional types established by his father, although with a cooler palette and a dryer line. Also by Carlo are two different interpretations of the *Adoration of the Magi.*

In the former Galería del Paseo of the Summer Palace, now Room Four, is a masterpiece by the Flemish artist Rogier van der Weyden, as well as various late 16th-century canvases by Italian and Spanish painters. These are closely connected to the decorative history of the Monastery or to the paintings collection which Philip II established there. Four of these —one by Veronese, another by Tintoretto and two more by Federico Zuccaro— were commissioned for the High Altar but were ultimately rejected as being iconographically unacceptable.

The Annunciation, signed by Veronese in 1583, forms a pair with the painting by Tintoretto and both seem to have been a specific commission. Its tight brushwork and line in comparison with Veronese's normal handling

PAOLO CALIARI, IL VERONESE   *ADORATION OF MAGI*

The Annunciation, 1583.

Seventh Room. Galería de Paseo. Summer Palace. King's House.

JUAN FERNÁNDEZ DE NAVARRETE "EL MUDO"

The Beheading of Saint James, 1571.

Seventh Room. Galería de Paseo. Summer Palace. King's House.

(Above) Juan van der Hamen y León
Two Still Lifes. Fruit and Birds in a Landscape,
1621 and 1623.
Fifth Room. Summer Palace. King's House.

(Right) Paolo Caliari, Il Veronese
The Annunciation, 1583.
Seventh Room. Galería de Pasco. Summer Palace.
King's House.

have led modern critics to doubt the attribution and to consider it a work-shop product, albeit with the intervention of a known collaborator. Tintoretto's *Nativity and the Adoration of the Shepherds* (the composition combines the two episodes) is a highly disputed work, which, if not by the workshop, is certainly not a wholly autograph piece.

Federico Zuccaro's *Adoration of the Magi,* painted in 1588, was rejected on the grounds that it did not place sufficient emphasis on the Virgin and Child. Zuccaro avoided this serious error in his *Nativity* of the same year but still included a basket of eggs which was not to the King's liking. However, according to Mulcahy, realistic details such as the basket or the dog or, on another level, the use of chiaroscuro, had a positive influence on the evolution of Spanish painting.

Among the paintings by the Riojan artist Juan Fernández de Navarrete, *El Mudo* (The Mute) are two surviving pictures from the series that made up his first major commission for the monastery. Both were so highly esteemed in the early 19th century that they were included in a group of pictures removed from El Escorial in 1810 in order to be sent to Paris. According to García-Frías, *The Penitent Saint Jerome,* signed and dated 1569, reflects Navarrete's early style in which his linear approach reveals his Italian training within the context of late Mannerism.

Signed and dated 1571, *The Beheading of St James* is Navarrete's most dramatic picture and a milestone in the development of Spanish art. The painter brings together the three iconographic aspects of the apostle, representing him as a Matamoros (Moor slayer) in the background and as a martyr in the foreground, as well as including the emblems of the Pilgrim. Mulcahy attempts to place these references to St James within the context of post-Lepanto triumphalism.

Among the works by Navarrete is a copy by Michel Coxcie of Van der Weyden's *Descent from the Cross,* paid for in 1569. The original work was formerly in El Escorial but is now in the Museo del Prado. According to Bermejo Martínez, Coxcie reproduces the original extremely closely apart from some differences in the colours.

Van der Weyden's superb *Calvary* hangs on one of the walls in the room. Most art historians put a fairly late date on the painting on account of the style, the grandeur of the composition and the chronological association with the Carthusian monastery of Scheut, near Brussels, to which the artist seems to have donated the work. Panofsky puts the date at 1462, two years before the death of the master. Bermejo Martínez dates it to around 1460-62 and states that the panel, which is exceptional for the period in its

large size and notable for its simple and highly effective composition, is the clearest manifestation of Van der Weyden's sculptural approach. It was restored in 1946-47.

On the opposite wall is *The Calling of Saint Saints Peter and Andrew* by Federico Barocci, one of a number of important gifts received by Philip II during his reign, as was *The Raising of the Daughter* of Jairus by Girolamo Muziano, a gift from Cardinal Montepulciano to the King, also on show in this room.

Room Five displays 17th-century Italian paintings, including works by Bolognese, Roman, Lombard and Neapolitan artists. In addition to *Jacob's Journey* by Andrea di Leone is an interesting portrait of *Innocent X with a Prelate* by Pietro Martire Neri, one of several signed versions that he made of the famous original by Velázquez of 1650. A distinctive feature of this version is that the artist depicted the pope full-length, accompanied by a relative. Particularly notable among the four paintings by Guercino is *Lot made drunk by his Daughters*. *Saint Augustine* and *Saint Monica* are by Guido Reni, while two versions of the *Mater Dolorosa* are by Stanzione and Sassoferrato.

The three inner rooms (Six, Seven and Eight) which look onto the Courtyard of the Masks feature 17th-century Spanish paintings. Room Six has works from the first half of the century, including paintings by Madrid artists contemporary with Velázquez. Notable here are a pair of *Still Lifes with Goldfinches* by Juan van der Hamen, and the *Birth of the Virgin,* by Jusepe Leonardo.

Room Seven contains more 17th-century works and focuses on Ribera and Zurbarán, as well as works by followers and workshop replicas. According to Mayer, *The Apparition of the Infant Christ to Saint Anthony,* attributed to Ribera, is a copy of the original signed and dated 1636 and now in the Real Academia de Bellas Artes de San Fernando in Madrid. Generally considered a workshop replica although with notable differences to the original, the restorations it has suffered now make it difficult to reach a definitive conclusion as to authorship. According to Juan Miguel Serrera, *The Presentation of the Virgin in the Temple* corresponds to an altarpiece commissioned from Zurbarán in 1629 by the Convent of the Trinidad Calzada in Seville. However, although executed under his direction, it is probably the work of collaborators.

Room Eight completes the display of Spanish paintings, concluding with artists of the High Baroque. The *Portrait of Mariana of Austria* is by Claudio Coello, as is the *Portrait of Mariana of Neuburg,* while Alonso Cano painted the *Virgin and sleeping Child* of ca. 1646-50 (one of his least inspired works in Wethey's opinion). Francisco Rizzi is represented by an *Annunciation* and the three *Floral Still Lifes* are by the still life painter Francisco Pérez Sierra who was highly esteemed by his contemporaries.

Room Nine was formerly Philip II's Summer Chamber, with was linked through his Bedroom via a galleried corridor with the projected lower church, ultimately completed and decorated as the Pantheon of Kings. It is now hung with numerous canvases by Luca Giordano who painted the ceiling frescoes of the Basilica and the Monastery staircase. These include a pair of saints, *Saint Jerome in Penitence* and *The Preaching of Saint John the Baptist,* as well as the Biblical subjects of *Samson between the Columns* and *Samson and the Poets*. Scenes from the life of Christ include the *Nativity*, the *Adoration of the Magi* and the *Ocaña Christ,* as well as a *Mary Magdalen.* The only non-religious painting is the *Portrait of Charles II,* the monarch who acquired numerous works by Giordano, later summoning him to Italy in 1692 where he commissioned the artist to execute various decorative and pictorial cycles.

The setting

The north-east corner of the Ladies' Tower from the balustrade of the dome of the Basilica.

East Façade.
The Queen's private garden seen from the windows of the Queen's Chamber or Infanta's Chamber.

THE GARDENS, THE KITCHEN GARDEN, AND THE FORGE MEADOW

The gardens are arranged over a terrace which is supported by seventy-seven arches, spreading out in front of the eastern and southern façades of the building. The so-called Wall of the Niches (its original name) has inset stairways and small caverns that give access to the kitchen garden. This wall provides the garden with an impressive architectural framework even by Italian standards. As well as resorting to the cliché of comparing the hanging gardens of El Escorial with the famous ones of Babylon, Father Sigüenza described its lower level as Roman.

Compartmentalized in accordance with the palace-monastery project, the outer zone comprises several gardens for different users. Three gardens surround the King's House; the northernmost was reserved for the courtiers and the rest belonged to the monks. The current image of boxwood rows stems from the eighteenth century although it has been very much altered by the growth of the vegetation. It retains little of the original design of squares of flowers in the Flemish style.

Work on the Wall of Niches began in 1570 but the completion and total finalisation of the supporting structure and its contents was a very slow process. According to Kubler, the double stairways leading from the garden in the royal residence to the lower park were not commissioned until 1583, while construction of the wall partitioning off the friars' recreation area took place in the following year.

Pairs of staircases descend to the kitchen garden. Here, we can admire the beautiful pond used for irrigation and fish farming designed by Francisco de Mora in 1588. He probably also designed the three rustic gateways in the Serlian Style which give access to this extensive area, completed in 1589. A very curious piece of architecture is the Cachicanía intended for the *cachicán* or gardener and taking the form of a square pavilion.

In the monastery's founding charter, mention is made of The Forge Meadow (*La dehesa de la herrería*) as early as 1564 as one of the assets that made up its splendid resources. This is still one of the most important landscape features of the architectural-natural surroundings of the monastery.

South Façade.

The Monks' Garden from the south arcade of

the Convalescents' Gallery or Sun Corridors.

La Lonja, the Staff Quarters, La Compaña, the House of the Infantes, the House of the Minister of State.

La Lonja or great L-shaped esplanade was constructed between 1586 and 1596 in front of the western and northern façades. Abutting the gardens, it traces a diagonal or bisecting axis superimposed on the frontal one of the palace-monastery. There are numerous examples of this contrary design within the extended context of Spanish architectural solutions. A gallery or underground passage was opened between the house and the Staff Quarters so that the staff in the service of the monarch would not be exposed to the strong winds that blew so fiercely across La Lonja. This was designed in 1769 by the Hieronymite architect Friar Antonio de San José Pontones, known as Padre Pontones.

The two buildings containing the servants' quarters were erected opposite the northern façade, skilfully negotiating a steep slope. These were constructed in 1587-88 by Juan de Herrera with a well-judged economy of means in order to house the king's servants. At the extreme south-western end of La Lonja, linked to the monastery through a walkway on arches is La Compaña which housed a wide variety of services for the Hieronymite community, including the stables, the workshops and the hospice or guest rooms. A very dignified building formally despite its functional purpose, construction started in 1580 based on a design attributed to Francisco de Mora.

Terminating La Lonja, the Infantes' House on the western side and, in line with the Casa de Oficios, the Ministry of State House, illustrate Juan de Villanueva's profound and innovate interpretation of Herreresque architecture based on strictly Neo-classical premises. The construction of the Infantes' House began in 1771 and was intended for the infantes' servants. The well-planned interior circulation system includes some notable staircases. These reappear in the house of the Minister of State or third Staff Residence, commissioned fourteen years later.

North Façade.
La Lonja with the 18th-century milestone: «6 1/2 leagues to Madrid and 1191 varas», and the Infantes' House in the background.

ANONYMOUS MADRID SCHOOL ARTIST, 17th-century.
View of the Royal Monastery of
San Lorenzo de El Escorial.
Ante-chamber of Philip II. King's Quarters.
King's House.

View of La Lonja with the north and main
or western façades of the Monastery.

JUAN DE VILLANUEVA

Casita del Infante or Casita de Arriba, 1771-73,

rear façade from the gardens.

The Casita de Arriba or Casita del Infante

The Casita was built between 1771 and 1773 for the Infante Don Gabriel de Borbón, son of Charles III, and was designed by Juan de Villanueva. It is located on a promontory known as the Dehesa de La Herrería and when seen from a distance presides over the gentle slope of the valley in which the monastery of El Escorial is situated, hence its name of the Casita de Arriba (Small Upper Palace).

Conceived as a typical recreational palace of centralised ground-plan, the main façade has a front portico or atrium with two Ionic columns beneath a Palladian entablature. This entrance, flanked by two Egyptian-style sphinxes which guard the approach formed by the courtyard in front of the building, has lost its original coherence due to changes to the perimeters and sculptural elements as well as the planting of conifers. These 19th-century alterations resulted in an aesthetic effect totally at odds with the original intimate concept of the design.

The rear façade opens onto the garden, which follows the formal, terraced model of Italian classical gardens, and is on two levels. The upper

Principal Salon, for chamber music concerts.

level is formed by the terrace terminating in an exedra which surrounds the palace and with whose axis it is aligned. Here we find a fountain and a table with eight stone seats in the style of a *belvedere* or viewpoint, and from this spot there are the finest views of the surrounding area with the Monastery in the distance. The lower, projecting terrace is square-shaped, decorated with rectangular box parterres. It descends from the side facades, following the line of the upper terrace wall, providing another vantage-point over the surrounding woodland.

The pavilion was designed for chamber music concerts as the Infante was a great devotee of music – Father Antonio Soler was one of his instructors – and for this reason the main, central Salon acts as a vestibule, an ample square space of double height crowned with an octagonal dome on flying vaulting, between which are galleries for the musicians, reached from the upper floor. The Infante and his guests thus enjoyed the music which drifted up to them from the lower floor of the main Salon or from just outside.

Sadly, none of the original decoration designed for the Casita has remained in situ and what can now be seen dates from the reigns of Charles IV to Alfonso XIII.

The fresco on the cupola of the main Salon, attributed to Vicente Gómez Novella, is painted with the *Four Seasons* alternating with oval windows, the whole connected with friezes and moulding which enclose coffering and representations of Classical subjects. In the centre of the Salon is a monumental gilt-bronze clock in the form of a Neo-classical octagonal temple on a terrestrial globe, an anonymous French work of the period. It stands on an Empire table of similar style in mahogany, its legs ornamented with swans and dolphins in gilt-bronze. On the walls are oil paintings with views of the Spanish eastern coastline by Mariano Sánchez Maella, and others of Royal Residences by Fernando Brambilla, alternating with mirrors above 18th-century console tables and Neo-classical chairs.

The door opposite the entrance leads into a room which looks onto the garden. The ceiling has simple modern painted decoration with motifs inspired by the *Berain* style divided up by bands of rosettes and cameos. From the ceiling hangs a 19th-century French light in crystal and gilt-bronze. This area leads on to the Saleta with its ceiling in the Pompeiian style, as well as to the Hunting Room or Office which has a 20th-century ceiling imitating Charles IV-period work with delicate grotesques interlaced with medallions against gold grounds and hunting scenes inspired by Paul de Vos. The furniture consists of Empire pieces in mahogany and gilt-bronze.

Through the side doors of the Vestibule we reach the Pompeiian Room and the so-called Bedchamber.

His Majesty the King, Don Juan Carlos, was the last member of the Spanish royal family to use this room as it was his residence while he was still a prince and studying at the Alfonso XII College in El Escorial.

Ceiling with a fresco of
The Four Seasons,
attributed to Vicente
Gómez Novella.
Principal Salon.

Vault with frescoes in the
Pompeiian style in the
Small Room.

JUAN DE VILLANUEVA
Casita del Príncipe or Casita
de Abajo, 1771-75 / 1781-84,
portico of the main façade.

THE CASITA DE ABAJO OR CASITA DEL PRÍNCIPE

This building was intended for the use of the Prince of Asturias, older brother of Don Gabriel and the future King Charles IV. It was built in an oak forest about half-way down the slope from the Monastery to the town of El Escorial, and is thus known as the "Lower" Palace.

The palace was constructed in two stages which its architect, Juan de Villanueva, was able to bring together in an exceptionally harmonious structure. Overall, it anticipates his ideas for the Royal Natural History Cabinet, the building which now houses the Prado Museum. In its first stage, from 1771 to 1775 and contemporary with the Casita del Infante, this little palace was built as a rectangular block with a porticoed façade measuring 27 metres long.

The second phase of 1781-84 saw the addition of a transverse wing which houses the Large Salon or Dining Room and the Oval Room, the latter opening onto the garden with a portico. Together they form a T-shaped ground-plan. Particularly notable is Villanueva's resolution of the graduation of the spaces between the main façade and the secondary ones and their conjunction with his formal garden, also inspired by Italian classicising models.

The entrance gateway, flanked by two sentry-boxes and a pair of porticoed pavilions, leads onto the square, chamfered courtyard which in Ferdinand VII's reign was planted out. This has a lower circular fountain in the centre.

In the background is the tetrastyle Doric portico of the raised central section of the main façade, joined to the two lateral, service wings by two porticoes with Tuscan columns. Thus the broad expanse of the main façade differentiates the east zone, facing the entrance from outside, from the intimacy of the garden hidden behind the western, rear façade, albeit relieving any uniformity through the use of different heights and levels and the opening of the linking porticoes onto the lateral wings of the garden.

In the rear garden the design follows the rising terrain, resulting in two different but interconnected spaces: the flat, square, lower area which surrounds the T-shape of the rear façade, ornamented with a simple fountain of chamfered profile in the centre of a box parterre. Above is the upper terrace reached through an attractive series of ramps and consisting of a broad area which terminates in an exedra with a square pond from which a little cascade falls down onto the lower area. Villanueva completed his decoration of the garden with fountains, benches and classical-style urns, but the delicacy of his design was rather obscured and spoiled by the large conifers planted in the 19th and 20th centuries.

The Casita del Príncipe is superior to that of the Infante not just for its more elaborate and sophisticated design but also because the interior decoration has been better preserved even though part of the original splendour was lost during the Peninsular Wars. Ferdinand VII again embellished it richly, but some of the most important works were moved to the Prado Museum or the Royal Palace in Madrid in order to avoid possible seizure during Carlist disputes. Eventually, during the reign of Alfonso XIII the frescoes were restored and the furniture now seen was installed (both restored again recently), reflecting something of the splendour of the original royal residence.

The larger rooms on the ground floor are decorated with frescoes (including the high

The Red Room.
Neo-classical furniture;
ceiling with frescoes in the
Etruscan style by
Vicente Gómez
18th century.

ceiling of the Tower Room on the first floor). These are in a variety of styles, including Pompeiian, inspired by the paintings found during the excavations at Pompeii, and Etruscan, in which ornamental and architectural elements predominate over figurative designs. These are by Vicente Gómez, the Court Painter whose work was highly valued for this type of project by Charles IV, and Manuel Pérez, his pupil and collaborator, as well as Juan de Mata Duque and Luigi Japelli. In another genre, Salvador Maella contributed his own style of pleasant allegorical works to the ceilings of the two staircases.

In contrast, on the upper floor where the ceilings are low, they are ornamented with fine stucco work in subtle and varied relief, partly painted in delicate colours with gilding, all executed by Giambattista Ferroni in Neo-classical style. The exceptions are the Dining Room or Main Salon and the Oval Room on the lower floor.

Initially, the flooring of the ground floor consisted of terracotta tiles that were covered according to custom and depending on the season of the year with rush matting or rugs. However, in the 20th century this was replaced with flooring of different inlaid coloured marble tiles arranged in geometrical designs. The staircase retains its old surface of different marbles and cut stones.

Upstairs we can still see the original flooring which is of exotic hardwoods of different colours and types inlaid to create foliate and geometrical designs. This wooden flooring is more appropriate to the small size of these rooms which were designed to house collections of objects made in delicate or precious materials.

This part of the palace houses the Porcelain Room with its 234 framed plaques in biscuit porcelain made at the Buen Retiro Royal Porcelain Manufactory in Madrid in 1790-95. They follow models by Wedgwood and were inspired by engravings of the excavations at Pompeii and Herculaneum sponsored by Charles VII of the Two Sicilies, the future Charles III of Spain. The adjacent Ivory Room is similar in approach and decoration to the preceding one, with 26 sculptures and ivory plaquettes, some of which were also made at the Buen Retiro Manufactory. The Portrait Room houses small portraits of members of the royal family during the reigns of Charles IV and Ferdinand VII.

The Embroidery Room is devoted to the textile arts and features 33 similarly remarkable embroidered pictures with borders. They are based on 17th and 18th-century paintings and made in a variety of colours and different stitches in silk thread by Juan López Robredo, Court Em-

Porcelain Room.

Royal Buen Retiro Madrid Porcelain Manufactory, 1790-95: framed plaques in biscuit porcelain.

Central plaque, *The Flood of Deucalion,* unleashed by Zeus to destroy the Earth as a consequence
of the crimes and impieties committed by the sons of Lycaeon (the Greek version of Noah's Flood).

TARAULT, PARIS: table clock. Alabaster. Second Empire, France, second half of the 19th century.

Pair of two alabaster amphorae, Neo-classical style, 19th-century.

broiderer to Queen Maria Luisa. Of similar style are the panels with borders of garlands surrounding small scenes and Pompeiian motifs which cover the walls and seats of the adjoining room, also called the Embroidery Room.

Finally, on the upper floor we reach the Tower Room and the Sofa Room (which has floral silk on the walls and on the canapé, the latter carved in exotic hardwoods after a design by Dugourc and from which the room takes it name). Here we should point out the textiles which are a feature of the rooms in the palace. Most of them retain the borders which edge the walls as well as some of their original silk wall hangings, en suite with the upholstery of the furniture. Some of these are documented, and were made in the Royal Workshops in Valencia (whose textile industry was then at its height), or were designed on commission from Jean-Démosthène Dugourc and woven at the Lyon manufactory of Camille Pernon for the Spanish royal residences of Charles IV and Maria Luisa. Together, they constitute a wide repertoire of floral and foliate motifs as well as designs based on the Antique in the Neo-classical and Empire styles.

With the exception of some pieces in the Ferdinand VII or Empire styles, most of the furniture is in late 18th-century style, particularly the Spanish Charles IV style. Within the context of the apparent uniformity and cold elegance of Neo-classicism, the results are sophisticated creations with numerous variations on the standard types: suites of console tables, seats, benches, canapés and matching fireplace screens, their designs differing according to the room for which they were intended. With these ends in mind, the Spanish Royal Workshops produced carved wood furniture of an unprecedented delicacy and brilliance of execution. Painted white and gilded for the ground floor, or veneered in mahogany and gilt-bronze for the upper, they constitute an exhaustive repertoire of ornamental possibilities derived from classical Antiquity.

Among these exceptional Charles IV pieces we should mention (in addition to the canapé referred to above) the large mahogany table in the Dining Room. This consists of a carved hard-stone top made at the Buen Retiro Royal Laboratory, supported on 16 Corinthian columns with gilt-bronze mounts resting on a marble base with mirrors which reflect the gilded, carved wooden coffering on the underside of the top.

Of the pictures hung throughout the palace, the majority are works by the Neapolitan artists Luca Giordano and Corrado Giaquinto, of mainly religious, allegorical and mythological subject-matter.

The rooms on the ground floor are arranged parallel to the transverse axis and to either side of the Vestibule. In the south wing on the left is the Sala Encarnada with its Etruscan-style ceiling by Vicente Gómez (who painted the ceiling of the Vestibule and the one immediately above it in the Tower Room); the Queen's Room with its ceiling fresco in shades of red by Manuel Pérez; the fresco by Pérez in the Sala del Barquillo, inspired by the *Aldobrandini Wedding* in the Vatican; and the Yellow Room, with its ceiling in a similar style to the red one in the Queen's Room. In the north wing on the right is the Sala de Tortillones, with bronze sculptures which are reduced-scale copies of works by Giambologna, while the ceiling is decorated with the *Labours of Hercules* by Juan Mata Duque. We also find the Japelli Room, named after the artist who frescoed the ceiling with an individual interpretation of the Pompeiian style involving grotesques alternating with broad architectural compositions filled with scenes of courtly life of the time.

In the adjacent side pavilion on the north side are three more ceilings painted by Vicente Gómez, filled with grotesques and medallions with allegorical and mythological subjects, while the walls are hung with a complete series of 18th-century engravings reproducing the Vatican *Loggie*, painted by Raphael and his pupils to decorate the papal apartments. Raphael's frescoes were extremely influential for the Neo-classical decorative arts, particularly for the so-called Charles IV style in Spain, and it is therefore not surprising that these prints were hung here at the time when the king had commissioned the construction and decoration of the Casita.

The longitudinal axis of the Doric portico gives onto the Vestibule of the reception rooms on the ground floor, originally comprising the main Salon before the enlargement of this perpendicular axis with the addition of the Dining Room and the Oval Room. This latter space, which opens onto the garden, has its ceiling and elliptical walls decorated with the finest stucco-work in the entire palace, consisting of partly gilded reliefs against painted borders alternating with sculptural motifs. These were executed by the brothers Domenico and Giuseppe Brilli with Giambattista Ferroni and surround the four niches with busts of Roman emperors.

Deception revealed,
18th-century.
Reduced-scale copy of the original marble sculpture by Francesco Queirolo for the Chapel of Santa Maria della Pietà, mausoleum of the Sangro family, princes of Sansevero, Naples.
Ivories Room.

MICHEL-ANGE HOUASSE

View of the Monastery of El Escorial,

from the north-east, c. 1720.

Patrimonio Nacional. Palace of La Moncloa.

The town

A Royal Decree of 28 April 1767 resulted in the development of the town next to the palace-monastery, and a suitable urban plan was devised by Juan Esteban. This was of very irregular format due to various pre-existing factors such as the terrain and Esteban's plan is less interesting than the town's houses which were built following Juan de Villanueva's guidelines over this configuration.

Among early surviving buildings it is worth mentioning the following: the Doctors' House (Casa de los Doctores) dating from 1583-85, built as a residence for the academics who gave classes at the Monastery College; the Casa de Jacometrezzo; the House of the Architect and the Church of Saint Barnabus by Francisco de Mora in the Lower Town. Eighteenth-century buildings include the Volunteers and Invalids' Barracks, most probably designed by Villanueva; the San Carlos Hospital, built around 1770 but rebuilt in the 20th century; the House of the French Consul, of the Marqués of Campo Villar, of the Merchants, and the Colonnade House by Villanueva, which retain their original design albeit with alterations in the form of additional floors or later enlargements. Also worth noting is the House of the Infantes Don Carlos María

Isidro and Don Francisco de Paula, dating from the reign of Charles IV and intended to house the Infantes' servants.

Another notable building is the Theatre or Real Coliseo constructed under Charles III in 1770-72 to a design by Jacques Marquet. It was considerably altered in the 19th century but has been restored and is in use today.

Of equal interest is the 16th-century water storage system which uses the so called "viaje grande" consisting of a system of vaulted stone arched structures through which the water enters and exits and is purified and filtered. The water comes from the springs of Puerto de San Juan de Malagón, location of the Arca de San Juan, from where it falls down through the force of gravity by means of a system of terracotta conduits interspersed with cleaning and registration tanks to join up with the waters from the Arca del Helechar or del Enebral, falling down to the third and architecturally more impressive tank known as the Romeral or Cascajal, then, once in the town itself, it entered the now lost reservoirs of the Caño Gordo or Repartimicntos. Finally, it arrived at the cisterns and storage tanks of the Monastery, the Compaña and the Casas de Oficios.

The degree of 1767 resulted in an increase in the number of buildings in the town in order to house the growing population made up of the aristocracy and their servants who descended on the town at the various times of year when the itinerant Court was present. This resulted in an increased demand for water which was met through the construction of the dams known as the Infante, the Romeral, the Batán and the Tovar. These had fallen out of use in the 20th century and the last three were therefore rebuilt, leaving only Villanueva's Infante dam, which had supplied water to the Casita de Arriba obsolete.

By a Royal Decree of 25 June 1792 Charles IV divided the Royal Residence into two completely differentiated areas: the Royal Residence of San Lorenzo and the Town of El Escorial.

In 1837, following the suppression of the Hieronymite community, the Monastery, together with its rural and town properties, reverted to the Crown.

Subsequently, the inauguration of the Northern Company railway line under Isabel II in 1861 launched a new era for the town and favoured its development as a summer location for Madrid residents. The town was now well connected to Madrid with easy transport of goods and people, allowing for the development of some industry and the creation of a working-class part of town with its interesting examples of late19[th]/early 20th-century urban industrial architecture.

With the 1868 Revolution a parallel process began by which Crown properties passed into private hands, including almost all of the urban centre of San Lorenzo and a third of El Escorial so that it passed out of the sphere or royal and ecclesiastical influence, the latter by now in complete decline.

New areas of town arose as a result of these sales, built on plots which had previously been occupied by various Crown buildings, such as the Colonia de Terreros and the area known as El Plantel. These were a response to the increasing numbers of visitors and summer guests as well as the permanent urban population.

The general European trend for villa and spa-hotel building close to royal residences evident in the late 19th and early 20th centuries was imitated in San Lorenzo with the construction of a number of private buildings. Stylistically, they followed the general historicist and eclectic styles of the time, albeit on a suitably modest scale.

Among the different types of buildings constructed in the town at this time were a number of single-family houses: some were rather cosmopolitan in style, with decorative whitewashed facades, while others had stone walls with brick panels, embellished with wooden balconies and glazed verandas, wrought or cast-iron decoration, crowned by pronounced gables in a style which fused the styles of contemporary central-European Alpine construction and 19th-century railway architecture.

Finally, from the mid-20th century, the progressive opening-up of transport and its increased speed, together with gradual improvements in average lifestyle have resulted in a ceaseless growth of the town which continues to the present day and includes the construction of new developments in the surrounding countryside.

Bibliography

BROWN, JONATHAN. *La Sala de Batallas de El Escorial: La obra de arte como artefacto cultural,* Universidad de Salamanca. Salamanca, 1998.

BURY, JOHN. *Juan de Herrera y El Escorial,* Patrimonio Nacional. Madrid, 1994.

BUSTAMANTE GARCÍA, AGUSTÍN. *La octava maravilla del mundo (Estudio histórico sobre El Escorial de Felipe II).* Editorial Alpuerto. Madrid, 1994.

CANO DE GARDOQUI Y GARCÍA, JOSÉ LUIS. *La construcción del Monasterio de El Escorial. Historia de una empresa arquitectónica.* Universidad de Valladolid. Salamanca, 1994.

GARCÍA-FRÍAS CHECA, CARMEN. *La pintura mural y de caballete en la Biblioteca del Real Monasterio de El Escorial.* Patrimonio Nacional. Madrid, 1991.

DI GIAMPAOLO, MARIO (coor.). *Los frescos italianos de El Escorial.* Sociedad Editorial Electa España. Madrid, 1994.

MULCAHY, ROSEMARIE. *The decoration of the Royal Basilica of El Escorial.* Cambridge University Press, 1994.
Spanish version: *"A la mayor gloria de Dios y el Rey": La decoración de la Real Basílica del Monasterio de El Escorial.* Patrimonio Nacional. Madrid, 1992.

VON DER OSTEN SACKEN, CORNELIA. *El Escorial. Estudio iconológico.* Xarait Ediciones. Bilbao, 1984.

RODRÍGUEZ ROBLEDO, PIEDAD. *Pedro de Tolosa, primer aparejador de cantería de El Escorial.* Colegio Oficial de Aparejadores y Arquitectos Técnicos de Madrid. Madrid, 1994.

RUIZ GÓMEZ, LETICIA. *Catálogo de las colecciones históricas de pintura veneciana del siglo XVI en el Real Monasterio de El Escorial.* Patrimonio Nacional. Madrid, 1991.

TAYLOR, RENÉ. "Architecture and magic: Considerations on the idea of the Escorial", in *Essays in the history of architecture in honor of Rudolf Wittkower.* Phaidon. London, 1967.
Spanish versions with revised and expanded text: Ediciones Siruela. Madrid, 1992.

WILKINSON-ZERNER, CATHERINE. *Juan de Herrera, architect to Philip II of Spain.* Yale University Press. New Haven and London, 1993.
Spanish version: *Juan de Herrera, arquitecto de Felipe II.* Ediciones Akal. Madrid, 1996.

Plans

Plans and designs based on Juan de Herrera´s original drawings *(Trazas)*, reproduced in Pedro Perret´s engravings.

Collado Villalva. Monasterio. Torre del Prado. Galapagar.

Las Aspleras.

CAMPILLO.

SCENOGRAPHIA

TOTIVS FABRICÆ

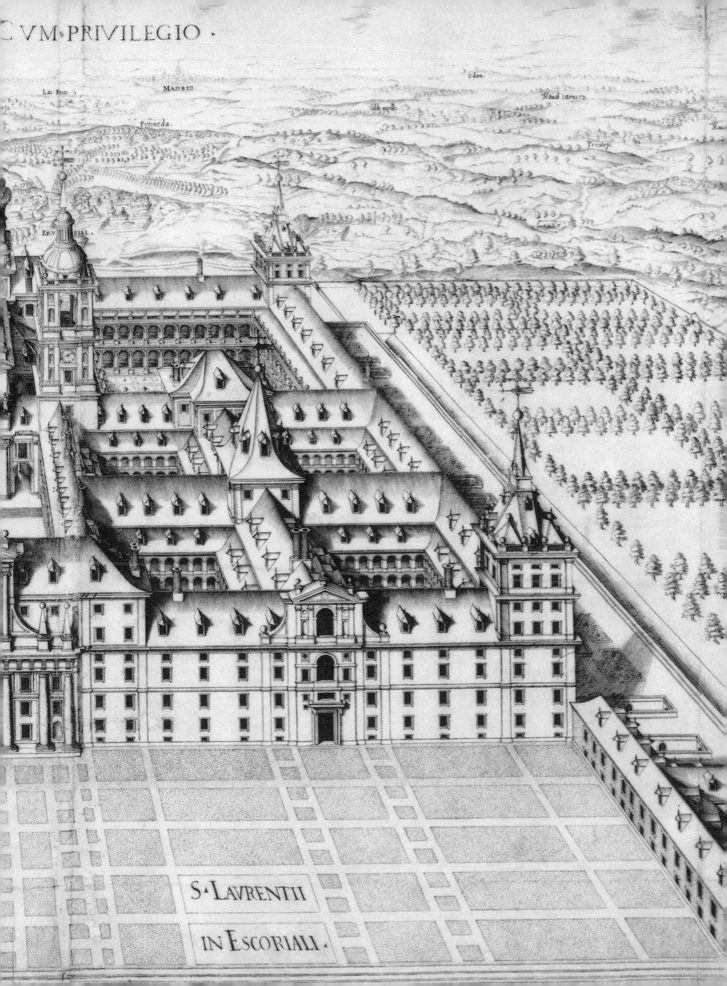

CVM PRIVILEGIO·

MADRID

S·LAVRENTII
IN ESCORIALI·